ETHICAL DIMENSIONS OF DIVERSITY

◩ Sage Series in Business Ethics

•

Series Editor: Robert A. Giacalone
The E. Claiborne Robins School of Business
University of Richmond

◩ Editorial Board

ETHICAL
DIMENSIONS
OF DIVERSITY

Willie E. Hopkins

 Sage Series on Business Ethics

 SAGE Publications
International Educational and Professional Publisher
Thousand Oaks   London   New Delhi

For information address:

SAGE Publications, Inc.
2455 Teller Road
Thousand Oaks, California 91320
E-mail: order@sagepub.com

SAGE Publications Ltd.
6 Bonhill Street
London EC2A 4PU
United Kingdom

SAGE Publications India Pvt. Ltd.
M-32 Market
Greater Kailash I
New Delhi 110 048 India

Printed in the United States of America

Library of Congress Cataloging-in-Publication Data

Hopkins, Willie Edward.
    Ethical dimensions of diversity / author, Willie E. Hopkins.
        p.   cm. — (Sage series in business ethics)
    Includes bibliographical references and index.
    ISBN 0-8039-7288-1 (acid-free). — ISBN 0-8039-7289-X (pbk. : acid
    -free)
    1. Diversity in the workplace. 2. Business ethics. I. Title.
    II. Series.
    HF5549.5.M5H67 1997
    658.3'008—dc21   96-45797

97 98 99 00 01 02 03 10 9 8 7 6 5 4 3 2 1

Acquiring Editor:	Marquita Flemming
Editorial Assistant:	Frances Borghi
Production Editor:	Michele Lingre
Production Assistant:	Karen Wiley
Copy Editor:	Joyce Kuhn
Typesetter:	Danielle Dillahunt
Indexer:	Christina Haley
Cover Designer:	Lesa Valdez
Print Buyer:	Anna Chin

Contents

Preface   ix

Acknowledgments   xv

PART I: Assessing the Ethics-Diversity Relationship

1. **Introduction**   3
   Ethics and Cultural Diversity:
      A Societal Perspective   4
   Ethics and Human Diversity:
      An Organizational Perspective   6
   Ethics and the Realities of Diversity   8
   Diversity and Ethics Paradigms   14

2. **Ethical Concepts and Diversity**   23
   Ethics as a Concept   24
   Moral Relativism and Diversity   27

3. **Ethical Values in Diverse Cultures**   34
   Cultural Value Systems   37
   Cultural Dimensions and Ethical Values   46

4. **Ethical Values and Diversity in Organizations**   55
   Corporate Culture and Ethics   57
   Ethical Codes in Organizations   59
   The Nature of Ethical Paradigms   61

5. Ethics, Diversity, and
   Organizational Performance   72
   Ethics and Organizational Performance   74

6. Managerial Ethics and Diversity   83
   The Ethnic Minority Perspective   84
   The White Male Perspective   86
   Cross-Cultural Perspectives   88
   The Legal Perspective   90
   The Role of Managerial Values   90
   Ethics, Diversity, and Managerial Effectiveness   92

7. Reconciling Diverse Ethical Values   94
   The Role of Human Resources Management   95

8. Implications for Business Ethics   105
   Business Social Responsibility to Diversity   107
   Business Social Responsiveness to Diversity   108
   Macro Solutions   110
   Micro Solutions   111
   Present Theories and Future Directions   112
   Future Challenges for Management   113

PART II: Cases in Ethics and Diversity   117

Case #1: Downsizing at Simtek   119
   Shirley A. Hopkins

Case #2: Chinese Values in American Society   122
   Winter Nie

Case #3: The Decision to Terminate Randy Shutz   125
   Willie E. Hopkins

Case #4: Performance Evaluation
   at Montana Trust & Savings Bank   128
   Shirley A. Hopkins

Case #5: Religious Warfare at Jones Consultants   132
   Shirley A. Hopkins

Case #6: Reconciling Diversity
   and Team Productivity at MSI-TECH   138
   Shirley A. Hopkins

Case #7: Hiring Decision At Medcom   142
   Shirley A. Hopkins

Case #8: Trouble on the Loading Dock   148
   Minnette A. Bumpus, David B. Balkin,
    and Wilfred J. Lucas

Case #9: Mark's Dilemma   151
   Shirley A. Hopkins

Case #10: Joe Foster's Rules   156
   Shirley A. Hopkins

References   161

Index   170

About the Author   182

About the Case Contributors   183

Preface

Ethical conduct, among individuals comprising the United States workforce, is governed by standards derived from "mainstream" American cultural values and moral traditions. In recent years, individuals from a variety of cultural, ethnic, racial, religious, and otherwise diverse backgrounds have been entering the United States workforce in record numbers. This trend is expected to continue beyond the year 2000. These diverse individuals will inevitably bring with them workplace behaviors influenced by cultural values and moral traditions that may be quite different from those held by mainstream America.

Increasing diversity in the U.S. workforce raises several ethics-related issues and questions. One issue raised is whether increased diversity in the workplace will lead to greater deviations from our corporate ethical standards. Another is whether U.S. corporations' codes of ethics can effectively govern employee ethical conduct under conditions of high workplace diversity. Will we see a shift in our corporate ethical standards as certain cultural, ethnic, or racial groups, whose ethical beliefs differ from mainstream America's, become a dominant force in the workplace?

Questions and issues such as these suggest that ethics, like science before it, may be undergoing a paradigm shift, and diversity rhetoric may be the harbinger. If there is such a monumental change afoot, what is its nature? Ought there be such a change? Moreover, in this rhetoric, diversity seems to be proposed as a value we have a moral obligation to promote. Ethics would ask its perennial questions: Is diversity a value? If so, what kind? Do we have a moral obligation to promote it? If so, how are we to proceed when it conflicts with other prima facie values? A major purpose of this book is to provide the reader

Visual Overview of Book

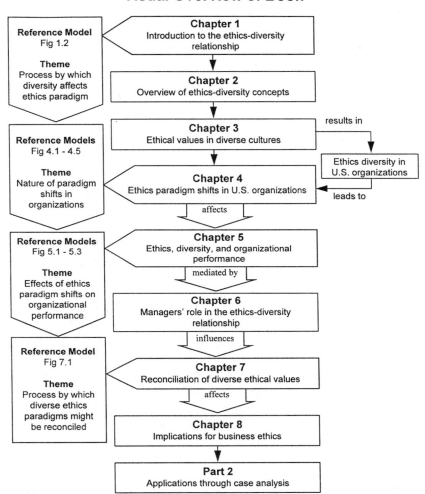

Reference Model Fig 1.2 **Theme** Process by which diversity affects ethics paradigm	**Chapter 1** Introduction to the ethics-diversity relationship
	Chapter 2 Overview of ethics-diversity concepts
Reference Models Fig 4.1 - 4.5 **Theme** Nature of paradigm shifts in organizations	**Chapter 3** Ethical values in diverse cultures
	Chapter 4 Ethics paradigm shifts in U.S. organizations
Reference Models Fig 5.1 - 5.3 **Theme** Effects of ethics paradigm shifts on organizational performance	**Chapter 5** Ethics, diversity, and organizational performance
	Chapter 6 Managers' role in the ethics-diversity relationship
Reference Model Fig 7.1 **Theme** Process by which diverse ethics paradigms might be reconciled	**Chapter 7** Reconciliation of diverse ethical values
	Chapter 8 Implications for business ethics
	Part 2 Applications through case analysis

results in

Ethics diversity in U.S. organizations

leads to

affects

mediated by

influences

affects

with practical guidelines for answering ethics-diversity-related questions such as these.

◩ USES AND OBJECTIVES OF THE BOOK

This book is designed to meet the educational and practical needs of students, teachers, business ethicists, and human resource professionals as they seek to better understand the relationship between different aspects of ethics and various dimensions of diversity. Designed as such, this book can be used in a variety of ways and in a variety of courses. In management of diversity courses, this book can be used as a primary text, and in business ethics and human resources courses this book can supplement the basic text when the instructor wants to provide students with a diversity perspective. For human resource professionals, this book can be used for purposes of consulting or as an ethics-diversity training manual. These uses are reflected in the following objectives.

1. *To provide the reader with multiple perspectives and viewpoints on understanding the ethics-diversity relationship*

This objective will be achieved by first relating various theories of ethics to an operational definition of diversity. Morally relevant dimensions of diversity are then identified for the purpose of learning something about diversity as a value notion in the current sociopolitical context. We then move to conceptual analyses of increasing diversity in the workplace and the impact it is currently having, and expected to have, on ethics paradigms in U.S. organizations.

2. *To provide the reader with a framework for going about deciding what one's general and specific obligations are with regard to diversity*

Against the backdrop provided by more theoretical discussions, this book presents practical guidelines for determining and fulfilling one's general and specific obligations toward diversity. By general moral obligations, we mean the general rules, attitudes, and strategies and perhaps some other things that an individual should adopt if acting in a situation of diversity. Specific obligations are the obligations we have, within the context of diversity, to make certain decisions and to act in certain ways. Besides these individual obligations, this book addresses the issue of corporate obligations and the probability that, to appropriately fulfill its moral obligations toward diversity, a corporation will likely have to go well beyond merely having an ethical code.

3. To enable the reader to progress from simply acquiring information about the ethics-diversity relationship to applying it within the context of diversity

There is no mechanical way to generate answers about how one should behave ethically within the context of diversity. Rather, those likely to be in such problem/conflict/dilemma situations stemming from diversity will need to develop practical skills that come from dealing with such situations regularly. The ethics-diversity cases provided in this book will afford the reader an opportunity to develop the analytical skills and human sensitivity that such situations require.

▧ ORGANIZATION OF THE BOOK

The book is divided into two parts. In the eight chapters comprising Part I, the "new" concept of diversity is interfaced with the "old" discipline of ethics (to include more recent developments). The progression of these chapters moves from theoretical discussions of ethics and diversity to discussions of how ethics-diversity concepts might be applied in practice. A visual overview of the book (see chart) shows the relationship between chapters and the general theme of each chapter. The reference models (i.e., figures) in Chapters 1, 4, 5, and 7 are conceptual models that relate to different aspects of the ethics-diversity relationship. These conceptual models show a progression of the relationship, beginning with the process by which increasing diversity "causes" a shift in organizations' ethics paradigms (Chapter 1), the nature of "diversity caused" paradigm shifts (Chapter 4), effects of paradigm shifts on organizational performance (Chapter 5), and the process by which diverse ethics paradigms might be reconciled (Chapter 7).

Chapter 1 defines the concept of diversity and ethics and discusses them from both societal and organizational perspectives. This chapter also presents a conceptual model of the relationship between ethics and diversity and provides discussions related to organizations' moral obligation toward diversity.

Chapter 2 begins by defining ethics as a concept and differentiating between ethics and several other ethics-related terms and concepts. The chapter continues by examining several ethics-related theories, within the context of diversity, and concludes with a preliminary discussion of the divergence of ethical frameworks in diverse cultures.

Chapter 3 explores the ethical values of groups and individuals from diverse backgrounds and cultures. This chapter speaks not only to normative differences among, say, Chinese, American, and Indian cultures but between women and ethnic minority differences as well. The chapter also provides a framework that allows organizations to assess the deontological norms of individuals and groups from diverse cultures.

Chapter 4 considers corporate codes of ethics and corporate culture as two ethics paradigms that determine ethical behavior in organizations. This chapter continues by examining the nature of ethics paradigms in organizations. It concludes by presenting a conceptual model, from which propositions are developed, concerning possible impacts of increasing diversity on organizations' ethics paradigms.

Chapter 5 focuses on the relationship between ethics and organizational performance. The mediating role of diversity in this relationship is explored with respect to its impact on corporate culture and strategy implementation. Discussions of the work ethic of individuals from diverse cultures and the implications for organizational performance round out this chapter.

Chapter 6 contains discussions related to managerial responses to increasing diversity and the ethical implications of these responses. These responses are considered from ethnic minority, white male, cross-cultural, and legal perspectives. It concludes with discussions of managerial values as they relate to diversity.

Chapter 7 contains a contingency framework for reconciling the ethical values that diverse individuals bring to the workforce. The primary focus is on the role that human resources management plays in this framework. The role of supervisory involvement and leadership is also explored within the context of contrasting views of whether behavior toward diversity can be regulated or reconciled.

Chapter 8 examines the ethical practices of business within the context of increasing diversity. Particular emphasis is placed on the social responsiveness of business toward diversity. Macro- and microsolutions to the moral mazes faced by business are recommended, as are recommendations for ethics-related research and practice as they relate to diversity.

Part II contains several cases that afford readers the opportunity to apply what they learned in the first eight chapters. The philosophy of Part II is that there are at least two ways of learning about the ethics-diversity relationship. One way is through the conceptual discussions provided in this book. The other is through practical application. It has been said that application is the highest level of learning. So, once the concepts discussed in this book have been understood, applying them to the cases in Part II should facilitate learning and understanding the ethics-diversity relationship. At the end of each case are two sets of discussion questions. The first set addresses ethical issues, and the second addresses human resources management (HRM) issues.

Acknowledgments

The efforts of many people contributed to the successful completion of this book. Without them, this book would not be possible.

The insightful comments and constructive suggestions of Barbara Parker of Seattle University, Ellen Ernst Kossek of Michigan State University, and Patricia Arredondo of Empowerment Workshops were instrumental in helping me improve the content quality of this book. My thanks and gratitude are extended to these reviewers.

The concepts set forth in this book are useless if one cannot apply them in some practical way. The cases, which were contributed by several of my colleagues, provide a practical way of applying these concepts. Thank you David, Minnette, Shirley, Wilfred, and Winter for sharing your valuable expertise.

I also thank Laurie Ray for preparing the tables and figures used in this book. And a very special thanks to my wife and colleague, Shirley, for her support and for keeping me organized during its preparation.

Finally, my sincere thanks to Marquita Flemming and the publishing staff at Sage. It has been a privilege and a pleasure working with all of you.

PART I

Assessing the Ethics-Diversity Relationship

Introduction

Since diversity is expected to characterize the workforce of the near future, we can no longer presume a common, universal, prevailing consensus for personal and organizational ethics.

S ocial philosophers are still debating the merits of encouraging members of a multicultural society to perpetuate their ethnic identities versus the merits of encouraging them to amalgamate into the "American melting pot." In recent years, this national debate has been dominated by a single theme: ethnic, racial, and social diversity. However, as groups other than those identified by race or ethnicity (e.g., feminists, homosexuals, the aged, and disabled individuals) intensify their efforts to be recognized as legitimate entities in America's mosaic of humanity, social philosophers have begun to move beyond the rhetoric of ethnic, racial, and cultural diversity and toward the new rhetoric of "diversity."[1]

Idiomatically, this new rhetoric has given rise to *ethnographic* descriptors such as nationality, religion, and language, *demographic* descriptors such as age, gender, and place of residence, *status* descriptors such as social, economic, and educational background, *sexual orientation* descriptors such as heterosexual, homosexual, or bisexual, and a range of other descriptors relating to formal or informal membership affiliations. Some of the major dimensions and descriptor variables used within the idiom of diversity are listed in Table 1.1. Beliefs are, among some, that wholesale subscription to the idiomatic rhetoric represented in this table will lead to a transmogrification of staples that have long been recognized as salient features of American society (e.g., high morals and enviable ethical standards). Are such beliefs warranted? Whether warranted or not, the outcome of the ethics-diversity debate may well be a redefinition of what constitutes the American character.

In this introductory chapter, we set forth some diversity- and ethics-related concepts and situations that will enable the reader to draw one's own conclusions as to whether or not beliefs about ethics-diversity relationships are warranted. We begin by looking at the ethics-diversity issue from both societal and organizational perspectives and then consider ethics and the realities of diversity. Specifically, the major groups subsumed under the general rubric of diversity are discussed with respect to their contribution to population growth in the United States and their participation in the U.S. workforce. The focus then shifts to explanations of an ethics-diversity process model and its components. This model affords the reader some theoretical insights into the ethics-diversity relationship and also provides a conceptual perspective of how the ethics paradigms of organizations might be altered as the level of diversity increases in their respective workforce. We conclude this chapter by offering some preliminary discussions of the moral obligations that organizations might have toward promoting diversity in the workplace.

▧ ETHICS AND CULTURAL DIVERSITY: A SOCIETAL PERSPECTIVE

Daniel Stein, executive director of the Federation for American Immigration Reform, is of the opinion that nations do not have the capacity to accommodate unlimited ranges of diversity (especially cultural) without irrevocably altering their own character (Aikman & Jackson, 1993). Let's focus on the ethical/moral character of America. (Although distinctions can be made between the terms ethics and morality, they are used interchangeably throughout this book.) Is it conceivable that the moral character of America will be altered if the range and magnitude of cultural diversity continues to increase

Table 1.1 Major Diversity Categories and Associated Descriptors

Category	Descriptors
Geography	Geographic diversity refers to an individual's affinity to or identification with a particular geographic location which may include, but is not limited to, the following: country, region, state, county, vicinity, rural, urban, suburban.
Culture	Cultural diversity refers to an individual's affinity to or identification with a particular cultural dimension which may include, but is not limited to, the following: race, ethnicity, nationality, color.
Gender	Gender diversity is usually limited to male and female.
Spirituality	Spiritual diversity refers to an individual's religious or spiritual affiliation which may include, but is not limited to, the following: Christian, Muslim, Jewish, agnostic, atheist, denominational, non-denominational.
Language	Language diversity refers to an individual's linguistic identity which may include, but is not limited to, the following: monolingual, bilingual, multilingual, dialectical.
Disability	Disability diversity refers to an individual's identification with some type of visible and/or invisible impairment which may include, but is not limited to, the following: physical, mental, visual, hearing.
Sexuality	Sexual diversity refers to an individual's sexual orientation which may include, but is not limited to, the following: heterosexual, homosexual, lesbian, bisexual, transsexual, transvestism.
Age	Age diversity refers to an individual's identification with a particular age category or generational nomenclature which may include, but is not limited to, the following: "twenty-somethings," "thirty-somethings," etc., "baby-boomers," "baby-busters," "generation X."

significantly and unchecked within the borders of the United States? If hordes of new immigrants flood America's shores and bring with them divergent ethical values and standards, will an ethical paradigm shift occur within American society? If we define ethics as the traditions of belief that have evolved over the years (or centuries) in societies concerning right and wrong behavior (Beauchamp & Bowie, 1983) and then apply this definition to the behavior of initiates to American society and subsequent responses to their behavior, the reader will gain additional insights from which conclusions about appropriate answers to questions such as these might be drawn.

We begin by considering the doctrine of cultural relativism, or the notion that what is right or wrong, good or bad, depends on one's cultural background. In other words, what is considered ethical in one society may be considered highly unethical in another. Now, consider the following events: In

1986, the district attorney of Dekalb County, Georgia, brought a Somali woman to trial for allegedly performing a clitoridectomy, which is a cultural tradition in some parts of Africa, on her 2-year-old niece. The reasoning was that such a tradition is not ethically or morally acceptable in American society. Four years later, however, the same district attorney decided not to press charges of child molestation against a South American woman suspected of stroking her male toddler's genitals, having concluded that "this is the way her culture taught her to put healthy young boys to sleep" (Lacayo, 1993).

Even though the behaviors of both women were wrong, based on the ethical/moral beliefs of American society, timing appears to be the major variable that determined each woman's fate. These events invites one to wonder whether charges would have been brought against the Somali woman had she committed the same "unethical/immoral act" in 1990 rather than in 1986. Did the district attorney relax his ethical/moral standards four years later to accommodate what he perceived as an ethical/moral paradigm shift in America due to the rapid infusion of diverse cultural values? Although an affirmative response to this question would not necessarily be indicative of a transmogrification of America's moral character, these events demonstrate the willingness of those through whom America's moral character is most often exhibited to alter this character (in the short term? permanently?) to accommodate cultural diversity.

▨ ETHICS AND HUMAN DIVERSITY: AN ORGANIZATIONAL PERSPECTIVE

The ethical character of organizations tend to reflect the ethical character of the society in which they are indigenous. Subsequently, those who believe that increasing cultural diversity will lead to a transmogrification of America's moral character also believe that increasing cultural and human diversity (e.g., the nonracial, nonethnic, noncultural components of diversity) will result in an ethics paradigm shift in Corporate America. The issue raised is whether or not these beliefs are grounded in reality. Current controversies surrounding homosexuals (a major human diversity category) in U.S. organizations provide enlightening insights into this issue.

In a recent article, it was reported that a high-level manager of a Shell Oil subsidiary accidently left a document in a copying machine that discussed rules for having safe sex at a homosexual party he was to attend (Stewart, 1993). The manager was not only fired but phony records were made up to indicate that he was terminated for reasons other than his homosexual lifestyle. This same article reported that in a 1987 survey conducted by the *Wall Street Journal,* 66% of major-company CEOs (chief executive officers) said they would be reluctant to put a homosexual on management committees. Yet in 1994, we find some of these same companies going so far as to offer health care benefits to the partners of homosexuals in their employment. Does this represent a change in organizations' view of what is morally acceptable?

Consider the situation at Apple Computer Company, where such a policy was recently adopted. During the week of December 6, 1993, Apple decided to cancel its plans to build a new customer support center near Austin, Texas. The decision was made after county commissioners rejected Apple's request for a $750,000 tax break because of the company's "pro-gay" benefits policy. Members of the commission expressed concern that such a policy would attract more homosexuals to the region, thereby altering the area's moral and family values (Swartz, 1993). However, during the week of December 13, 1993, the commissioners voted 3-2 to approve the tax break. They relented in response to negative public opinion, generated by the potential loss of 1,450 new jobs that the Apple facility promised to create (Cole, 1993).

Although this situation represents a clear case of negative publicity (driven by economic concerns) overshadowing moral ambiguities, the recognition of a diverse element in Apple's workforce initiated events that shaped the situation. In a more recent case, Coors Brewing Company joined Apple in offering full benefits to homosexual companions ("Coors Extends," 1995). The move surprised gay and lesbian groups and others who considered the brewer a bedrock of conservative values. Perhaps as an harbinger of things to come, lawyer and constitutional scholar Laurence Tribe wrote a brief that persuaded the United States Supreme Court (by a 6-3 vote) to invalidate the anti-gay-rights Amendment 2 to Colorado's constitution (Toobin, 1996). To be inferred from this surprising Supreme Court decision and the other organizational incidents previously cited is that staunch opposition to what is perceived by some as aberrations from America's traditional moral standards may be giving way to a new tolerance toward the diverse values and ethical standards that will inevitably permeate a highly diverse workforce.

▨ ETHICS AND THE REALITIES OF DIVERSITY

The American motto "E pluribus unum" might be loosely defined as one society composed of many different groups of people. In noting the way in which so many different groups in the United States are able to preserve their separate identities, historian Daniel Boorstin suggests that the motto should be "E pluribus plura" (Elson, 1993). Along this same line, historian Arthur M. Schlesinger, Jr. is of the opinion that the diversity dogma belittles "unum" and glorifies "pluribus" (Jamieson & Seaman, 1993). The term "pluribus" is derived from the word pluralism, which is defined in *Webster's New Collegiate Dictionary* as a state of society in which members of diverse ethnic, racial, religious, or social groups maintain an autonomous participation in and development of their traditional culture or special interest within the confines of a common civilization.

The message conveyed by these definitions and commentaries is a belief that the pluralist underpinnings of human diversity may lead to a fragmentation of the centrist consensus of what constitutes the host of ethical/moral values that many still consider vital to the American character. Later in this chapter we set forth a conceptual model of the ethics-diversity relationship that focuses on the ethical/moral values of organizations that might be affected by increasing levels of human diversity in their respective workforces. In the following pages, however, we look more closely at the different groups (at least the major ones) that are subsumed under the general rubric of human diversity.

As we look at these different groups, an assumption made is that each group contributes its own ethical/moral character to American society. A corollary assumption is that each group will bring to the workplace varying ideas of what is right and what is wrong. Knowledge of the parameters that define each group (e.g., numbers, dispersion patterns, attitudes, and perhaps even physiognomy) may provide insights into whether and to what extent each group's participation in American society, and thus in U.S. organizations, is likely to influence existing ethics/moral paradigms.

Immigrants

The top 10 ancestry groups that have immigrated to the United States as of fiscal year 1992 and the top 10 countries of origin for recent immigrants are

Table 1.2 Major Cultural Groups of the United States (As of Fiscal Year 1992)

Top 10 Ancestry Groups		Top 10 Countries of Origin for Immigrants	
	(in millions)		(in percentages)
German	58	Mexico	22.0
Irish	39	Vietnam	8.0
English	33	Philippines	6.3
African	24	Soviet Union	4.5
Italian	15	Dominican Republic	4.3
Mexican	12	China	4.0
French	10	India	3.8
Polish	9	El Salvador	2.7
Native American	9	Poland	2.6
Dutch	6	United Kingdom	2.1

SOURCE: 1992 statistical yearbook of the Immigration and Naturalization Service.

shown in Table 1.2. The information provided in this table reveals the extent and significance of immigration in the United States and suggests that immigration accounts for an increasing percentage of population growth in the United States. Indeed, between 1960 and 1970, immigrants represented 11% of total population growth; between 1970 and 1980, 33%; and between 1980 and 1990, 39% (U.S. Bureau of the Census, 1992).

In terms of legal immigration, more than 1 million people are admitted to the United States every year. From 1983 through 1992, 8.7 million immigrants were admitted—the highest number in any 10-year period since 1910. A record 1.8 million were granted permanent residence in 1991. Also, because present immigration law stresses family unification, the spouses, sons, and daughters of these new residents are virtually assured of gaining admittance to the United States; approximately 3.5 million are waiting to be admitted under these conditions (Aikman & Jackson, 1993). The information provided in Table 1.3 indicates the areas of the world where the majority of these legal immigrants are coming from as well as the number of individuals immigrating from these areas over the past several years.

Table 1.3 Sources amd Patterns of Immigration Over the Years

Years	Major Sources			
	Europe	Asia	Mexico	Caribbean Central America South America
1929	158,598	40,154	40,154	9,572
1990-92	393,027	1,054,069	1,839,037	888,817

With passage of the Immigration Act of 1990, which is indicative of a more liberal U.S. immigration policy, the numbers shown in Table 1.3 will likely increase significantly in years to come. Something worth mentioning about the numbers shown in this table is that, whereas most of the cultural groups immigrating to the United States in the past were from Europe, the majority of immigrants currently being admitted represent cultural groups from Asia, the Caribbean, Mexico, and Central and South America. To be inferred from this shift in immigration patterns is that one can expect a plethora of divergent ethical values to permeate the workplace of the future. Finally, the numbers in Table 1.3 do not reflect the number of illegal immigrants and asylum seekers entering the United States each year. Although no one really knows the numbers, estimates have been placed at 300,000 a year currently and almost 5 million over the past 10 years. In terms of asylum seekers, U.S. applications were up to 103,000 in 1992, and the backlog is well over 300,000 (Aikman & Jackson, 1993).

The map provided in Figure 1.1 shows where immigrants entering the United States are expected to settle during the 1990s. The implication of the numbers shown on this map is that most states can expect to experience moderate to high immigration growth throughout the decade. Also, because many of these immigrants will become immediate participants in the U.S. workforce, organizations conducting business in these states can expect an increase in the number of immigrants in their respective workforces. The result will be a culturally diverse workplace in terms of culture, race, and ethnicity as well as a host of diverse ethical values and moral standards. What effect, if any, will the values, beliefs, attitudes, and behaviors of individuals from these diverse cultures have on the ethics paradigms of U.S. organizations?

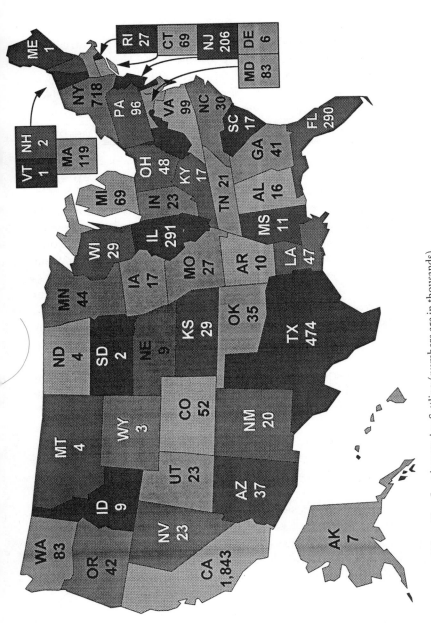

Figure 1.1. Where New Immigrants Are Settling (numbers are in thousands)
SOURCE: 1992 statistical yearbook of the Immigration and Naturalization Service.

11

Ethnic Minorities

Along with immigrants, ethnic minorities (including Hispanic Americans, Asian Americans, Native Americans, and African Americans) are contributing to significant population and workforce growth in the United States. For example, Hispanic Americans, who represented 24 million people and 9% of the United States population in 1992, are expected to increase to 81 million and 21% by 2050 and become the largest minority group in America; African Americans, 32 million and 12% in 1992, are expected to increase to 62 million and 16% by the same year; Asian Americans, 8 million and 3% in 1992, are expected to increase to 41 million and 11%; and Native Americans, 2 million and 1% in 1992, are expected to increase to 5 million and slightly over 1% (Blonston, 1992).

Ethnic minorities are also expected to enter the U.S. workforce in record numbers between now and the year 2000 (Johnston & Packer, 1987). Between 1980 and 1990, for instance, there was a 1.9% increase in the number of Hispanic Americans participating in the workforce, a 1.6% increase in the number of Asian Americans, and a .7% increase in the number of African Americans (U.S. Bureau of Labor Statistics, 1991). Although ethnic minorities are entering the workforce in record numbers, women are expected to dominate the workplace in the 21st century. In 1992, 47% of all workers in America were women, and they are expected to absorb 64% of all new jobs created by the turn of the century (Zeiger, 1992). As a reflection of this, there was a 3% increase in the number of women participating in the workforce between 1980 and 1990 (U.S. Bureau of Labor Statistics, 1991). As a group, they represent the highest percentage of new entrants to the U.S. workforce. Physiognomically, the typical new entrant to the workforce is expected to be a mature woman, probably an immigrant, whose first language is not English (Zeiger, 1992).

Thus, women, minorities, and immigrants are predicted to represent 85% of all new entrants to the U.S. workforce between now and the year 2000 (Johnston & Packer, 1987). The shifting dynamics of the workforce have placed managers, many of whom are white males, in a moral quandary. In their efforts to accommodate increasing diversity in the workplace, they will certainly be faced with the decision to hire or promote women, minorities, and immigrants over white males who may be morally outraged by these developments. Will these managers be able to effectively reconcile the personal ethical conflicts that will inevitably arise from decisions about hiring, firing, and promoting in a highly diverse workforce? Will the motivation to reconcile these conflicts lead to an alteration of their personal or their organization's ethics paradigms?

Age Groups

The "baby boomers" (individuals born between 1946 and 1961) and the "baby busters" (individuals born between 1968 and 1971) are age groups that must receive major consideration in the human diversity debate. The median age of the workforce, which was 28 in 1970, will be almost 40 by the year 2000. The number of workers older than 45 will increase by 30%, making most of the workforce middle-aged in less than a decade (Jamieson & O'Mara, 1991). These older individuals, classified as "baby boomers," have shaped much of postwar America's moral and ethical values. Although they see themselves as unique individuals, they tend to share a number of values as a group that contrast significantly with those of the previous generation. Moreover, they differ from the previous generation in their dedication to defining their personal ethical and moral values and living in accordance with them (Mills & Cannon, 1989). They are also much more likely than the previous generation to impose their values on subsequent generations—mainly, the "baby busters" (Zinn, Power, Yang, Cuneo, & Ross, 1992).

Baby busters represent 46 million Americans, aged 18 to 29, who make up the vanguard of the next generation. Alternatively called "Generation X," baby busters are the first generation of latchkey children who are products of dual-career households or, in some 50% of cases, of divorced or separated parents. Because they are such a racially diverse group (e.g., 14% African American, 12.3% Hispanic American, and 3.9% Asian American, compared with 12.4%, 9.5%, and 3.3%, respectively, for the entire population), they are more comfortable with diversity than any previous generation (Zinn et al., 1992). Because individuals in this group consider themselves alienated by a culture dominated by baby boomers for as long as they can remember, they pride themselves in rebelling against the "morally superior" values subscribed to by the baby boomers. As individuals from "Generation X" begin to dominate the workforce, what impact will they have on the ethics paradigms established by the baby boomers?

Homosexuals

Although Census Bureau figures are not conclusive, Overlooked Opinions, a Chicago-based market research firm, estimates that there are nearly 25 million gay and lesbian adults in the United States (Miller, 1992). Despite the size and buying power of this group, which is estimated to be over $514 billion annually (Johnson, 1993), discrimination on the basis of sexual orientation is still legal in much of the United States and practiced in many organizations. In 1991, for example, Lockheed Corporation (prior to its merger with Martin Marietta) allowed a Christian Fellowship group to use company facilities but not a group of gay and lesbian employees that had "come out of the closet" at this organization (Stewart, 1991).

Sexual orientation is by far the most sensitive diversity issue, provoking the most intense discussions because it centers on sex and touches on religious and moral beliefs. Positioned between the "family values" right, mainstream marketing efforts to gain a share of their combined annual income of $514 billion, and activist efforts to win them acceptance in Corporate America, homosexuals are presenting a moral challenge to American society. Even though most are still "in the closet," they are three times more likely than the average American to hold professional or managerial positions. As they fight their way out of the "closet" and begin to use the influence of their powerful positions, will we see a shift in the moral and ethical values of mainstream Corporate America?

◪ DIVERSITY AND ETHICS PARADIGMS

The census and labor force statistics cited above support Jamieson and O'Mara's (1992) assertion that "the workforce of the near future will display only one major characteristic: diversity. . . . The workforce will be a technicolor tapestry of ethnicity, gender, age, education, skills, abilities, attitudes and expectations" (p. 68). Inevitably, individuals comprising this diverse workforce will bring to the workplace varying ideas of what constitutes morally right and wrong behavior. Although organizations may have ethical codes that specify right and wrong behavior, a relevant issue is whether these codes can effectively govern employee ethical behavior under conditions of high workplace diversity.

Another issue concerns whether or not organizational codes should even attempt to govern employees' ethical behavior. After all, as some critics contend, only the individual employee can be responsible for one's own behavior (Velasquez, 1983). The contention is that employees make decisions about their individual behavior; organizations do not. Does this mean that organizations are not morally responsible for anything they do? If not, then the responsibility for ethical behavior is on the individual employee, not the organization or the ethical codes created to govern employee behavior. Evidently, individuals from different cultures do not believe that organizations should attempt to govern employees' ethical behavior by instituting ethical codes.

Consider the sentiment of a French employee of an American corporation toward such codes:

> I resent having notions of right and wrong boiled down to a checklist. I come from a nation whose ethical traditions date back hundreds of years. Its values have been transmitted to me by church and through my family. I don't need to be told by some American lawyers how I should conduct myself in my business activities. (cited in Vogel, 1992, p. 35)

It probably is safe to assume that employees from diverse cultural, ethnic, and racial backgrounds hold similar sentiments. If they do not subscribe to such codes, can their ethical and moral behavior be effectively influenced by them? If they feel that these codes are inappropriate or inconsistent with their personal codes, will they make a conscious or unconscious effort to alter them?

Although Americans tend to emphasize the role of the individual as the most critical source of ethical values, ethical behavior among individuals comprising the United States workforce is governed by standards derived from mainstream American cultural values and moral traditions (Vogel, 1992). As we have seen, however, individuals from a variety of cultural, ethnic, racial, and otherwise diverse backgrounds have been entering the United States workforce in record numbers. These diverse individuals bring with them workplace behaviors influenced by cultural values and moral traditions that may be quite different from those held by mainstream America. In fact, there is empirical evidence that cultural diversity is related to ethical diversity (Cohen, Pant, &

Sharp, 1992), meaning that there are as many different ethical and moral standards as there are different cultures.

Increasing diversity in the U.S. workforce raises several ethics-related issues and questions. One such issue is whether increasing diversity in the workplace will lead to a shift in Corporate America's ethics paradigm. In other words, will we see a change in Corporate America's ethical and moral standards as different cultural, ethnic, racial, and interest groups, whose ethical and moral beliefs may be in conflict with mainstream America's, become a dominant force in the workplace? As individuals and groups from diverse cultures and back-grounds enter the workplace, they will not automatically shed their ethical and moral values at the door. The issue becomes whether, and to what extent, their ethical and moral values will alter existing ethics paradigms in organizations. The conceptual model shown in Figure 1.2 suggests a process by which increasing diversity in the workplace might affect an organization's ethics paradigm.

An Ethics-Diversity Process Model

As indicated in Figure 1.2, increasing diversity in an organization's work-force will likely create additional communication and value differences that management must reconcile. If these differences cannot be reconciled rapidly and effectively, they will likely affect the efficient functioning of what might be called an organization's "cultural network." A cultural network that functions efficiently stabilizes the corporate culture, and a stable corporate culture de-termines the nature of the ethics paradigm that exists in organizations. The relationship between diversity and ethics will become clearer as we define the terms and concepts set forth in the model. Let's start by defining what we mean by the concept of an ethics paradigm.

Ethics Paradigm

The concept of an ethics paradigm might be defined as those formal or informal moral standards adopted by organizations to ensure that the behavior engaged in by individuals, during the pursuit of achieving organizational objectives, does not violate organizational values. The function of the paradigm is to translate organizational values into the types of behaviors that support the values. In short, the paradigm serves to protect the value and, therefore, the integrity of the organization (Karp & Abramms, 1992). It is noted here that we are referring to a descriptive ethics paradigm. In other words, no attempt is

Figure 1.2. A Process Model of the Ethics-Diversity Relationship

made to pass judgment on the superiority or inferiority of the ethical codes or systems that are operative in organizations. We choose to emphasize descriptive ethics because it is neutral and does not advocate one set of values and beliefs over another, but merely states that a certain set of values and ethics seems to be dominant in organizations (Buchholz, 1989).

Corporate Culture

This concept has been described in the following way: "The corporation is a community with a culture and value commitments. As a community it is an organizational context of persons and groups; a system of customs, expectations, values, and purposes; and a system of action and interactions" (McCoy, 1985, p. 63). Along with this description, corporate culture has been defined as the pattern of shared values and beliefs that give employees meaning and provide them with rules for behavior in their respective organization (Davis, 1985). Defined as such, corporate culture is the main vehicle for communicating, teaching, and enforcing the ethical values and standards that exist in organizations (Robin & Reidenbach, 1989). It has been suggested that a strong, stable corporate culture is capable of harmonizing divergent ethical and moral values that may exist in organizations (Frederick, Davis, & Post, 1988).

Cultural Network

According to Gerloff (1985), a "cultural network" is the mechanism that stabilizes the corporate culture of organization. This network, which is an aspect of "social information processing," produces strongly shared values, beliefs, attitudes, and behaviors throughout the organization. Communication and organizational-individual value differences, arising from increases in workforce diversity, may affect this cultural network. That is, these differences are likely to affect the social information processing that must occur to facilitate the efficient functioning of the network.

Communication Differences

In U.S. organizations, the ethical and moral values that guide employee workplace behaviors are conveyed primarily in the English language. Employees must be able to clearly understand the verbal, nonverbal, and written messages they receive via the cultural network that teaches and enforces the ethical values and standards subscribed to by organizations. As the workplace becomes more diverse, however, English may be spoken as a second language by many individuals. In fact, there are currently more than 140 different languages and dialects spoken in the United States, and over 11% of the population speaks a language other than English at home (Getter & Alvarez, 1994; Soloman, 1993).

Although individuals from diverse cultures and backgrounds will likely have at least minimal proficiency in the English language when they enter the workplace, the cultural context in which these individuals were raised will determine their capacity to clearly understand messages they will receive through the cultural network. For example, in a study of communication in high-context and low-context cultures, it was reported that

a high-context communication or message is one in which most of the information is either in the physical context or internalized in the person, while very little is in the coded, explicitly transmitted part of the message. . . . A low-context communication is just the opposite; i.e., the mass of information is vested in the explicit code. . . . Although no culture exists exclusively at one end of the scale, some are high while others are low. (Hall, 1981, p 48)

To be inferred from this statement is that in high-context cultures much of the meaning in communications is derived from the paralanguage, facial expressions, setting, and timing. Alternatively, in low-context cultures, the literal words chosen convey much more of the meaning in communication (Boyacigiller & Adler, 1991). As more and more culturally and linguistically diverse individuals enter the workplace, the efficient functioning of the cultural network is likely to be affected. In turn, this will affect the stability of corporate culture. If the corporate culture cannot effectively transmit ethical values and ensure adherence to "morally prescribed" behavior in a culturally diverse workplace, the ethics paradigm it supports will be affected in some manner.

Value Differences

Individuals and groups within organizations must share in a set of "core values" and norms to promote coherent behavior toward achieving organizational objectives (Schein, 1984). These values, which are transmitted through the organization's cultural network, brings stability to corporate culture. Individuals from diverse backgrounds will bring diverse values to the workplace. To minimize disruptions to corporate culture, these diverse values must be rapidly reconciled to the core values subscribed to by organizations. However, empirical studies have found that it can take several years for the values of culturally diverse individuals to be reconciled to the core values of organizations (Hopkins & Hopkins, 1990).

Besides this effect, some groups in a diverse workforce may challenge the validity of these core values and act purposefully to modify or supplant them with their own. As a result, the efficient functioning of the cultural network will likely be affected which in turn will affect the stability of corporate culture. The actions of gay activists across the country are beginning to affect the cultural networks, and thus the corporate culture, of organizations whose core values do not correspond with their agenda to (a) make discrimination according to sexual orientation as impermissible as discrimination according to race, age, or gender; (b) promote "diversity training" to encourage workplace tolerance toward gays; and (c) lobby for benefits that heterosexuals enjoy, mainly health insurance for partners (Stewart, 1991).

Explanations of the components comprising the model shown in Figure 1.2 provides a clearer picture of the process by which increasing diversity in the workforce is likely to affect ethics paradigms in organizations. If an assumption is made that this model accurately reflects the relationship between increasing diversity and ethics paradigms in organizations, can organizations experiencing increasing diversity in their workforce expect some type of shift in their ethics paradigm? If so, will their ethical standards be relaxed to accommodate diverse values, even though the values may be in conflict with those subscribed to by organizations? Will these diverse values be incorporated into the existing values subscribed to by organizations, such that their corporate codes of ethics are modified to reflect this incorporation? Questions such as these raise other questions. For example, if there is a shift in the ethics paradigms of organizations, attributable to increasing diversity, what will be the nature of this shift? Based on current presuppositions about the inherent nature of diversity, might inferences be drawn concerning the potential nature of the shift?

Presuppositions About Diversity

Arguments for promoting diversity in the workplace seem to presuppose another reason beyond the traditional fairness reasons, namely, that diversity itself is good. Is this presupposition warranted? If diversity is good, what kind of good is it? In itself? As a means? If it is a prima facie good, can we successfully adjudicate cases in which it comes into conflict with other prima facie goods (e.g., fairness or efficiency)? These questions must be answered antecedently and abstractly before we can even speculate about the nature of shifts in the ethics paradigms of organizations, attributable to increasing diversity.

If the presupposition that diversity is good is not warranted, should one assume that diversity is inherently "bad," and that this trait will determine the nature of any shift in the ethics paradigms of organizations? Would management in organizations be morally or legally justified in discouraging diversity through discriminatory actions? That is, would management actions be morally or legally justified if presuppositions that diversity is inherently bad are factual? One might argue successfully that management would have a moral justification for discriminating under such a condition. However, the results of diversity-related cases that have been adjudicated in the past provide compelling evidence that discrimination under almost any condition is illegal.

Discrimination is not only illegal, but discrimination lawsuits can be very expensive. For example, State Farm Insurance settled a class-action discrimination suit for $300 million, General Motors settled a similar suit for $40 million, and US Corp. settled a class-action discrimination suit for $42 million. On a smaller yet still impressive scale, Northwest Airlines settled a racial discrimination suit for $1.2 million, a sexual harassment suit cost K Mart three times that amount, and Pillsbury settled a similar suit for $1.76 million. It has been estimated that diversity-related lawsuits can cost the offending organizations, on average, $75,000 (Gordon, 1992).

Moral Obligations Toward Diversity

The examples cited above clearly suggest that whether one presupposes that diversity is inherently good or bad, organizations have a legal obligation toward diversity. An issue raised, however, is whether they have a moral obligation toward diversity. The resolution of issues concerning the moral obligation of organizations toward diversity requires one to accept a broader definition of ethics: one that goes beyond questions of good or bad, right and wrong. As defined earlier, ethics is a discipline for dealing with questions of good or bad, right and wrong. However, in the minds of many executives and ethicists, there is a broader definition of ethics that encompasses issues of social responsibility. (Philosophers might call these superogatory duties.) Issues like bribery and insider trading clearly accord with traditional definitions of ethics, but diversity-related issues must be addressed through the application of this broader definition.

Many executives, for instance, believe that organizations have a social and moral obligation to promote diversity. The rationale is that if business organizations have a social responsibility to increase their profits (Friedman, 1970) and if a diverse workforce will help organizations be more competitive and thus more profitable, then organizations are being socially responsible as well as fulfilling a moral obligation by promoting diversity. On the other hand, there are some who feel that organizations do not have a moral obligation to promote diversity. The feeling is that whether the goal is equal performance (in terms of competitiveness and profitability) or superior performance, the way to achieve this goal is to stop treating diversity as a moral issue and start treating it as a business issue (Gordon, 1992).

However, it might be argued that these two issues are inextricably linked. For example, social responsibility is fundamentally an ethical concept, and the term *responsibility* has moral overtones implying that business organizations have an obligation to someone or something. Therefore, when organizations engage in socially responsible behavior by promoting diversity, they are not only addressing a business issue but a moral issue as well. Moreover, whether they act voluntarily or in response to societal or regulatory pressures, when organizations act in a socially responsible manner toward diversity they are essentially demonstrating their moral if not legal obligation to diversity.

Issues and Ethics-Related Concepts

The nature of diversity and the rate at which it is occurring in the workplace of U.S. organizations will no doubt raise issues of ethics in a highly diverse workplace to new levels of concern. Many of these issues, expressed in the form of questions, have been raised in this introductory chapter. Discussions provided here have addressed, albeit briefly, some of these issues. Several ethics-related concepts were also introduced in this chapter. Some were explicitly defined and others implicitly defined within the context of discussions. In Chapter 2, ethics-related concepts that are directly related to the types of diversity discussed in this book are explicitly defined within the context of diversity.

◥ NOTE

1. With respect to political correctness, "America" refers to South, Central, and North America. In this book, however, America is used in reference to the United States of America.

2

Ethical Concepts and Diversity

If we are to understand the nature of ethics in a diverse workforce, we must first learn something about the different streams of ethical thought and examine them within the context of diversity.

Although the concept of diversity was explained in some detail in Chapter 1, many of the ethics-related concepts were simply introduced without much definition. Moreover, strong connections were not made between diversity and the ethics-related concepts that were introduced. In this chapter, the focus is on those ethics-related concepts most relevant to the types of diversity described in this book. The intent of this chapter is to define these concepts in such a way that a clearer picture of the ethics-diversity relationship is developed. The first few sections of this chapter focus on the fundamental concepts of ethics, values, and morality. Later sections focus on the ethics-related concepts of moral relativism, utilitarianism, justice, and rights that relate more directly to diversity in the workplace.

▨ ETHICS AS A CONCEPT

The concept of ethics is derived from the Greek word *ethos,* which has been loosely translated as meaning internal character (Byron, 1977). Consistent with this translation, ethics has been defined as

> a process by which individuals, social groups, and societies evaluate their actions from the perspective of moral principles and values. This evaluation may be on the basis of traditional convictions, of ideals sought, of goals desired, of moral laws to be obeyed, or of an improved quality of relations among humans and with the environment. When we speak of "ethics" and ethical reflection, we mean the activity of applying these various yardsticks to the actions of persons and groups. (McCoy, 1975, p. 2)

A general inference to be drawn from this definition, which is analytical in nature, is that ethics focuses on human activity done knowingly and to a large extent willingly. However, in this book the term is used in reference to either descriptive or prescriptive ethics. As mentioned in Chapter 1, descriptive ethics does not pass judgment on the superiority or inferiority of the ethical systems operative in different cultures or societies. No set of values or beliefs is advocated over another; only factual descriptions of moral behavior and values in various cultures and societies are described. The ethical values that are operative in diverse cultures are described in Chapter 3. In contrast to descriptive ethics, prescriptive or normative ethics is not morally neutral. It is concerned with the formulation of moral norms governing moral life and setting forth a particular set of standards that is best for people to adhere to. The models presented in Chapter 7 represent applications of prescriptive ethics. Chapter 7 focuses on the interplay of managerial ethics and diversity and seeks to reconcile any points of conflict through prescriptive approaches.

Ethics and Values

Although the terms "ethics" and "values" are often used interchangeably, distinctions can be made between the two concepts. One distinction is that ethics tends to focus on the conduct of individuals, whereas values represent the fundamental beliefs that individuals hold about conduct (Rokeach, 1968). In other words, values are the underlying beliefs and attitudes that help determine conduct. Distinctions made between these two concepts suggest that rather than viewing them as interchangeable their relationship might be better described as interdependent. Such a view is supported by ethicists who see the function of an ethic as one of translating any value into behaviors that support that value (Karp & Abramms, 1992). Ethicists who support such a view espouse the following relationship between values and ethics:

Values	Ethics
Define the individual	Translate values into actions
Are constant	Are changing
Are internally derived	Are situationally determined
Are concerned with virtue	Are concerned with justice
Are general	Are highly specific
Are stated morally	Are stated behaviorally
Are judged good or bad	Are judged there or absent
Set priorities	Set boundaries for behavior

Among the many things suggested by the juxtaposition of these two concepts is that (a) a value establishes for an individual a moral standard for taking an action that is designed to achieve some goal and (b) the purpose of an ethic is to ensure that an action that is designed to achieve a certain goal will do so without violating a value. With respect to diversity, it is possible for individuals from different racial, cultural, ethnic, or otherwise diverse backgrounds to hold the same moral values but to behave differently when faced with a common ethical situation. This is because of the reasoning process through which they apply externally imposed ethical codes (Buller, Kohls, & Anderson, 1991). Consequently, their personal moral values may be violated by applying ethical codes formulated by the organization. From an organizational perspective, the issue becomes how good or bad the consequences of this violation might be for the employee(s) involved and the implications that these consequences may hold for the organization.

Ethics and Morality

The concept of morals or morality is also often used interchangeably with ethics. Whereas *ethos* in the Greek is translated into what we call internal character, the Latin translation of *ethos* is *mos, moris,* from which the term moral is derived (Byron, 1977), shifts the emphasis from internal character to actions (i.e., external behavior, acts, habits, and customs). From a psychologist's point of view (Best, 1992), the issue of morality centers around four action-oriented questions:

- How does an individual interpret situations, and how does that person view any possible action as affecting others' welfare?
- How does an individual figure out what the morally ideal course of action should be?
- How does an individual decide what to do?
- Does the individual implement what he or she intends to do?

The action orientation of morality places it under the umbrella of what is called *teleology*. Teleological theories of ethics hold that whether an act is morally right or wrong depends solely on how good or bad the consequences of the action are for oneself. Stated somewhat differently, the teleological perspective on ethics argues that acts are morally right or good if they produce some desired state of goodness or pleasure and are morally wrong or bad if they produce some undesirable state of badness or pain. Subsequently, the rightness or wrongness of actions is determined by the results that these actions produce and not the act itself.

As a distinguishing point, morality is concerned with actions, and ethics is more concerned with setting boundaries for appropriate action. In normative terms, then, ethics is associated with a branch of moral philosophy called *deontology*. (By normative, it is meant that this approach to ethics seeks to uncover, develop, and justify the basic moral principles or values of a moral system.) Deontological theories of ethics emphasize that ethical standards should be based on principles, laws, rules, and other duties that lie outside oneself rather than on the goodness or badness of the consequences for the individual (Pettit, Vaught, & Pulley, 1990). Advanced by the work of Kant, these theories focus on universal statements of right and wrong concerning the duties of individuals (Kant, 1964). Derived from the word "duty," deontological or normative ethics is simply that duty (i.e., to conduct oneself ethically) is a requirement, and the burden of proof lies with any exception to it.

These two categories of theories (teleological and deontological) as they relate to ethics and morality become particularly important within the context of diversity. For example, teleology proposes that individuals from diverse backgrounds may hold the same moral values but may behave differently when faced with a common ethical situation, and deontology proposes that ethical standards should be based on externally imposed rules. The relevance here is that American organizations tend to define ethics in terms of rules, checklists, principles, and guidelines for individuals to follow in distinguishing right from wrong (Vogel, 1992). Yet, as will be seen later in this book, not all individuals from diverse backgrounds appreciate having notions of right and wrong boiled down to a checklist of rules. Although they may be expected to hold the same moral values (as proscribed by the organization's code of ethics), their interpretation and subsequent response to this externally imposed code may differ significantly.

▧ MORAL RELATIVISM AND DIVERSITY

In normative terms, when any two individual cultures have differences regarding the morality of a particular action or behavior, both can be right because morality is relative. This sense of moral relativism suggests that absolute notions of good or bad and right or wrong are not valid. Rather, there exist certain factors that make notions of morality relative to some personal or cultural standard (Gifford, 1983). Subsequently, moral relativism can create severe practical difficulties in organizations with high levels of diversity in their workforce because such a wide variety of conflicts among gender, racial, and ethnic groups can arise during the course of normal interaction (Nemetz & Christensen, 1996; Wolin, 1993). Four subforms of moral relativism (individual, role, social group, and cultural) are relevant to the types of diversity discussed in this book. These subforms are particularly relevant to discussions related to potential impacts that increasing diversity may have on existing ethics paradigms in organizations. Each subform is discussed below.

Individual Relativism

This subform of moral relativism subscribes to the view that what is right or wrong or good or bad depends on the feelings or attitudes of the individual. If a person feels that taking a bribe is wrong, then the practice of bribing is wrong for that individual. If another person believes that this practice is not wrong, then taking a bribe is not wrong for that individual. According to this doctrine, each individual is ultimately responsible for one's own actions, and we (society? the organization? management?) must let each make moral decisions according to one's personal standards (Gifford, 1983).

Essentially, those who subscribe to this doctrine conclude that because of the personal and serious nature of ethics and the fact that we are ultimately responsible for our own actions, each individual is the sole judge of what actions are morally correct; no one else has the right to judge. Such a view requires that one be tolerant of all individuals regardless of how their actions affect us (Wisdom, 1970). The relevance of tolerance in a diverse workforce comes into play only if management subscribes to the doctrine of individual relativism and only if it is taken to the extreme. As stated in Chapter 1, as individuals from different cultural, racial, ethnic, and otherwise diverse backgrounds enter the workplace they will undoubtedly bring with them varying ideas of what is right and what is wrong. Subsequently, managerial tolerance of individual relativism may well lead to a shift in the organization's ethics paradigm. Whether this shift is positive or negative will depend on the extent to which management is able and willing to resolve ethical conflict within the context of diversity.

Role Relativism

This subform of moral relativism proposes that a society can be viewed as a set of social roles that must be occupied by individuals. Viewed as such, morality becomes a matter of properly defining these roles and the obligations attached to them (Goffman, 1981). According to some ethicists (e.g., Freeman & Gilbert, 1988), values give substance to an individual, and the individual can adopt roles only in the context of one's own values—values shaped by the culture or environment in which that individual was raised. Within the context of diversity, then, it is highly likely that individuals will adopt roles based on the values instilled in them by their native culture or native environment rather than on the values of the host country (or organization) in which they live (or work).

The implications for diversity's impact on organizations' ethics paradigms will likely manifest themselves when such individuals are faced with an ethical situation that may affect the organization. When individuals ponder the question of what they should do in such a situation, role relativism would dictate that they do what is required by their role. If that role is determined by values other than those that are consistent with organizational values, a violation of the organization's ethics paradigm will occur. The issue, however, is whether a preponderance of such occurrences in a highly diverse workforce will eventually lead to a shift in the organization's ethics paradigm. As an accommodation to diversity, the possibility exists that such a shift might occur.

Social Group Relativism

This subform of moral relativism suggests that an individual's actions should not be judged as morally wrong if such actions are accepted practice by that person's relevant social group. Within the context of workforce diversity, moral conflicts may arise for individuals from collectivist societies. In such societies, individuals feel they owe absolute loyalty to their social group (e.g., family, friends). In return for taking actions deemed acceptable by the group, the individual is protected by the group. Conflict is likely to arise in organizations when the actions taken by such an individual is accepted by that person's social group but goes against what is morally acceptable by the organization in which the individual is employed.

In terms of social group relativism, morality is simply a matter of following the norms that are accepted practice. The issue, however, is whether individuals in a highly diverse workforce are able to withstand the internal and external pressure to adhere to their social group's acceptable practices when they are also obligated to adhere to a code of ethics that requires them to follow practices acceptable only to the organization that supports their livelihood. Again, will a preponderance of such occurrences in a highly diverse workforce eventually lead to a shift in an organization's ethics paradigm? This is a question that organizations will have to answer as their workforce becomes more diverse.

Cultural Relativism

Viewed as a slightly more sophisticated version of social group relativism, cultural relativism is the doctrine that what is right or wrong or good or bad depends on one's culture. This doctrine sets forth the belief that morality is relative to groups and individuals that make up a culture and, therefore, no universal norms exist that apply to all people and all cultures (Beauchamp, 1982). The following propositions represent the compound thoughts of those who subscribe to the doctrine of cultural relativism:

1. Different cultures have different moral codes.
2. There is no objective standard that can be used to judge one cultural code better than another.

3. The moral code of American culture has no special status; it is merely one among many.

4. There is no "universal truth" in ethics; that is, there are no moral truths that hold for all peoples at all times.

5. The moral code of a culture determines what is right within that culture; that is, if the moral code of a culture says that a certain action is right, then that action is right, at least within that culture.

6. It is arrogant for us (Americans) to judge the conduct of other peoples. We should adopt an attitude of tolerance toward the practices of other cultures.

An interrogatory statement that sums up these propositions might be this: If the moral standards of a culture are a product of its customs that have developed over a long period of time, what right does some outsider have to say "That action is morally wrong, even though it is within the bounds of your culture's moral standards"? Within the context of multinational ethics, where the principle of "when in Rome do as the Romans do" applies, these propositions seem a reasonable position to adopt. This is particularly true of Propositions 5 and 6, which suggest that certain actions may be right within that particular culture and that we should adopt an attitude of tolerance toward the practices of other cultures. However, within the context of diversity in U.S. organizations, these propositions (and the interrogatory statement that summarizes them) appear to be in conflict.

The conflict arises when the organization's workforce becomes more diverse. Management may feel that the behavior brought to the workplace by these diverse individuals may be morally correct within their culture but not in the culture in which management must attempt to lead and motivate and yet is expected to adopt an attitude of tolerance toward the behavior. The conflict is heightened by the cultural relativist notion that the organization must be "all things to all people." This notion is essentially an admonition against moral imperialism, imposing one's morality on others, or judging them by standards which they do not accept. As the workforce of U.S. organizations becomes more diverse, the concept of cultural relativism will figure prominently in the ethical debate. In this book, the debate centers on the implications that applications of this concept might hold for ethics paradigms in U.S. organizations and the role that diversity might play in any shifts that might occur in these paradigms.

Utilitarianism, Justice, and Rights

These ethics-related concepts also have direct implications for diversity. For the most part, these concepts are most relevant to managers who must make decisions within the context of diversity. For example, utilitarianism holds the view that whether an action is right or wrong depends on the good or bad consequences produced for everyone affected by the action. Although the goal of utilitarianism is to provide the greatest good for the greatest number, managers who hold utilitarian attitudes may (consciously or unconsciously) sacrifice the welfare of minorities (including women and individuals from various racial, ethnic, and cultural groups) in the interest of the majority—mainly white males.

Situations where a white male manager decides to lay off women and minorities during an economic downturn, because such an action will improve job security for white male employees, may not only be discriminatory but illustrate how a utilitarian decision can result in bad consequences in the interest of producing the greatest good for the greatest number. It has been found that many U.S. managers hold utilitarian attitudes toward ethical behavior (Fritzsche & Becker, 1984). This research finding is not surprising as such attitudes are consistent with managers' productivity goals. Thus, laying off women and minorities, who may be perceived to be less productive than white males, might be morally justified from a utilitarian perspective.

The concept of "justice" has two aspects that are relevant to diversity: distributive justice and procedural justice. *Distributive justice* calls upon managers to impose and enforce organizational rules and policies fairly and impartially, and *procedural justice* considers whether proper procedures have been followed during the distribution of benefits and burdens among organizational members (Rawls, 1971). With respect to diversity, the focus of distributive and procedural justice is on the degree to which employees are treated the same (according to guiding rules and standards) regardless of individual characteristics based on ethnicity, race, gender, age, or other particularistic criteria (Schermerhorn, 1993).

Closely associated with the concept of justice is the concept of rights. Within the context of diversity, this concept suggests that individuals (regardless of race, gender, etc.) are legally entitled to free and equal access to any rights guaranteed them by law. As stated by Wood (1990), however, "The concept of rights tells us only that employees have rights; it does not tell us how those rights should be balanced in practical management situations" (p. 207). In her book on the "rights" of employees in the workplace, Patricia Werhane (1985) sets forth a number of rights that she believes are necessary for both employers and employees if the concepts of distributive and procedural justice are to be carried out effectively in a diverse workforce. Of these rights, three apply most directly to diversity-ethics interface:

- Every person has an equal right to a job and a right to equal consideration at the job. Employees may not be discriminated against on the basis of religion, sex, ethnic origin, race, color, or economic background.
- Every employee has the right to free expression in the workplace. This includes the right to object to corporate acts that he or she finds illegal or immoral without retaliation or penalty.
- Employees shall be expected to carry out job assignments for which they are hired unless these conflict with common moral standards or unless they were not fully informed about these assignments or their dangers before accepting employment.

In a general sense, the concept of rights and the other concepts discussed in this chapter are interrelated, particularly as they relate to diversity. The relationship will become clearer as you read through each chapter in this book. Either explicitly or implicitly, you will encounter the various ethics-related concepts discussed in this chapter. For the most part, however, the concepts of moral relativism (including the subforms of individual, role, social group, and cultural), utilitarianism, justice (including distributive and procedural), and rights in the workplace applies mostly to material presented in Chapter 6. The focus of Chapter 6 is be on linking ethics with managerial behavior toward diversity in the workplace. In Part 2 of this book, these concepts are applied through case analyses.

The Origins of Ethical Frameworks

By examining ethics-related concepts within the context of diversity, it becomes clear that there is a divergence of ethical frameworks in place around the world. One might also infer from such an examination that there may be some fundamental consensus regarding these frameworks. For instance, Frederick (1985) states that

> embedded within humankind are moral meanings and conceptions of what is felt to be ethical. Great systems of thought, whether Christian, Marxist, or humanist, have captured portions of these moral meanings. These moral notions—they could be called moral archetypes—comprise the most fundamental, deeply felt value orientations of humankind generally. Each society varies its emphasis upon the rudimentary moral meaning but each returns over and over again to the basic structure of morality inherent in human interactions. Human behavior occurs within a web of such moral meaning and cannot escape being judged in terms of such a culture of ethics. (p. 16)

This statement supports the existence of divergence as well as consensus of ethical frameworks within the context of diverse cultures. When discussing diversity and the impact it might possibly have on existing ethics paradigms in organizations, the tendency is to focus first on differences in the frameworks before considering how they might be reconciled. As will be seen in Chapter 3 of this book, differences in the political, economic, religious, educational, and technological environments that individuals and groups reside in influence the formation of their ethics and value system. Greater understanding of these determinants at the individual and societal levels will provide better insights into the ethics-diversity relationship.

3

Ethical Values in Diverse Cultures

Ethical values are a result of a culture's unique history and traditions. Therefore, what is considered ethical in one culture may be considered unethical in another.

In the introductory chapter to this book, corporate culture was recognized as a major determinant of how employees behave, more or less ethically, in U.S. organizations. However, it has been suggested that with the influx of groups and individuals from different countries, the corporate culture of U.S. organizations may well become nothing more than shifting coalitions of subcultures with ethical values that are deeply rooted in their particular national, racial, and religious culture (Hofstede, Nevijen, & Sanders, 1990; Schein, 1983; Sinclair, 1993). Cultural theorists have suggested that these different subcultures are more likely than corporate culture to be the repository of values and norms that have lasting and significant influences on ethical behavior in organizations (Martin & Siehl, 1983; Sinclair, 1993; Wilkins & Ouchi, 1983). A strong conclusion that one might draw from suggestions made by cultural theorists is that these subcultures are sources of ethical discourse and dialectic as well as ethical conflict in organizations.

Instead of attempting to impose corporate-derived ethical values on its various subcultures, the task of organizations becomes one of understanding and unleashing the moral commitment of these subcultures toward goals that are consistent with those of the organization. For organizations to complete this task, the first step they must take is to develop an understanding of the different subcultures, of the terrain of existing ethics and values, and the points of difference between organizational ethics and values systems and those introduced by the different subcultures (Gregory, 1983). By developing this understanding, points of potential consensus can be developed and this can be the basis of a core of ethics for the organization (Arogyaswamy & Byles, 1987). As a basis for this understanding, it has been recommended that the acknowledgment of points of differences between subcultures should also include a tolerance for their diversity (Hodgson, 1992). With respect to the racially, ethnically, and culturally diverse individuals comprising these subcultures, this recommendation implies that American managers should subscribe to the notion that Western values, beliefs, customs, and ethics are not the only acceptable ones.

This recommendation also recognizes that many cultures have value systems that did not evolve from Greco-Roman and Anglo-Saxon roots. Indeed, most other value systems were established centuries before the United States existed. To be sure, the values and customs of other cultures are not necessarily primitive, degraded, or wrong because they are different from those subscribed to by Western culture. The point conveyed by this recommendation is that American managers can no longer presume a common, universal, prevailing consensus for personal and corporate ethics. In other words, they can no longer assume that all employees, even those indigenous to the United States and especially those from diverse cultural, racial, and ethnic backgrounds, ascribe to some single, all-encompassing ethical code.

As some ethicists contend, neither academic philosophy, religious morality, nor legal proscriptions command the kind of definitive, universal authority that we once thought they had (Primeaux, 1992). Subsequently, there is a need to recognize cultural, racial, and ethnic differences and to realize how these differences relate directly to differences in ethics and values. There is also a need to chart the origin and growth of these differences. As a starting point, it has been suggested that American managers know the historical, ethnic, cultural, political, legal, and religious facts about diverse groups, as these facts influence the way people think, interact, and behave. In this chapter, we explore some of the cultural factors that influence the ethical values of diverse groups and individuals in organizations. The superordinate influence of religion on their ethical values, within the context of deontology, receives particular attention. Fundamental to the dogma of deontology is the belief in the inherent rightness of behavior. For example, Buddhism, Hinduism, Judaism, Islam, and Christianity adhere to sets of rules that esteem certain immutable ethical standards.

Religion frequently enters discussions of ethical values because throughout most of human history, the determination of what was right or wrong was based on what was considered pleasing to the gods (Pettit et al., 1990). In many cultures, religion still plays a role in this determination. In both Jewish and Islamic religions, for example, the accumulation of wealth is regarded as a gift from God (McHugh, 1988). Subsequently, achieving financial success is a value that is encouraged by members of Jewish and Muslim cultures. Although most Protestant religions would not condemn this "accumulation of wealth" value, a warning about the evils of greed would likely be included with the acceptance of such a value in Christian faiths.

In Western society, the determination of what is morally right or wrong is generally based on the Bible and what is considered to be the will of the Judeo-Christian god, Yahweh. America's dependence on religious principles for moral guidance is highlighted in its first president George Washington's "Farewell Address" to the nation, in which he wrote that "reason and experience both forbid us to expect that national morality can prevail in exclusion of religious principles" (cited in Evans, 1994, p. 86). However, not all who subscribe to Christian religious principles set forth in the Christian Bible take direction from these principles. For instance, in an assessment of what the ethical paradigms of Western culture's middle managers would possibly be like in the year 2015, a sample of American high school students (future middle managers) was asked who they view as the greatest authority in matters of absolute truth. The majority responded "Me." This response might be interpreted to mean that there is no source of ethical or moral authority beyond their own experience. In other words, the Christian influence has virtually disappeared, and there is no indication that young people in America acquire a coherent or consistent value system from religion. Religion notwithstanding, it appears that in modern societies the responsibility for determining right from wrong rests more with the individual and the collective conscience of cultural members.

As the value systems of different cultures are discussed in this chapter, the influence of religion on the ethical values of individuals raised in these cultures will become apparent. Although we will consider the influence of religion and other factors on the ethical values of indigenous subcultures (e.g., ethnic minorities and women in U.S. organizations), the major focus of this chapter is on cultural diversity, specifically on the ethical values of various cultural clusters (i.e., countries and regions with overlapping cultures) and comparing them to the ethical values subscribed to by mainstream America.

▧ CULTURAL VALUE SYSTEMS

The fine points of the definition and components of culture are often debated. Those involved in the this debate, though, would probably agree that culture involves a pattern of values, beliefs, and behavior of a society or group. Most would also agree that although the discrete components may not be unique to a culture their combination and pattern are. Using a framework for assessing the values of different cultures, Mary Munter (1993) demonstrated its utility by comparing American values and the values of Muslim-based cultures on the "nature" and "time" orientations proposed in the framework. Once her comparisons were made, Munter concluded that internal control ("nature") and a future orientation toward "time" are reflected in American values systems and that external control and a past orientation toward time is reflected in Muslim-based value systems. To support her conclusion, Munter pointed out that what an American might view as a perfectly reasonable goal, such as completing a project on schedule, a Muslim might view as irreligious because Muslims believe that human efforts are determined by the will of Allah, not by a schedule.

As the value systems of different cultural clusters are discussed in this chapter, several cultural themes (e.g., nature, time, social relations, activity, and humanity) and dimensions (e.g., customs, traditions, and religion) will emerge. Their influence on the deontological ethics of groups and individuals from diverse cultures will become apparent as you read through this chapter. With respect to cultural clusters, a number have been identified in the literature. However, discussions of value systems presented in this chapter are limited to Asian, Latin, and European clusters (see De Cenzo, 1988, for a full discussion of different cultural clusters). As indicated in Chapter 1 (see Table 1.3), individuals from these cultural clusters represent the greatest proportion of the total number of culturally diverse groups immigrating to the United States. In the latter part of this chapter, a more comprehensive sample of cultural clusters is presented. This sample, combined with a more specific set of cultural dimensions, is then used to derive a practical framework for assessing the deontological norms of groups and individuals from different cultures within an organizational context. Also discussed are the value systems of Japanese, East Indian, and Australian cultures because each has unique aspects that warrant inclusion in discussions of diverse cultural values.

The Asian Value System in General[1]

The Koreans, Japanese, and Chinese have distinct cultures. Yet they are connected by a common social philosophy stretching back many centuries. In fact, this social philosophy has spread across Asia, extending to Indonesia, Malaysia, India, Taiwan, the Philippines, Thailand, and other Asian countries where intercultural migration has occurred. A common thread woven through these Asian cultures is the strong influence of dominant religions such as Confucianism, Taoism, and others in the countries of Chinese descent and of Buddhism and Shintoism in Japan. A value stressed by these religions is social interaction, which is the basis of the strong group identification, formality and courtesy, modesty, humility, and taciturn demeanor for which Asian cultures are known.

In Asian organizations, the prevailing values espoused by corporate culture are "loyalty," "accommodation," and "honoring authority." For example, the founder of Korea's largest family-run conglomerate, Samsung, wrote an employee policy in 1938 explaining that loyalty to the organization would be highly valued in all employees. Similar policies related to this loyalty value exist in most Asian organizations. In terms of the accommodation value, Asian employees often seek to minimize dissent. This value ensures that confrontations are avoided and that statements are carefully worded to avoid hurting the feelings of others. The loyalty and accommodation values exit in the shadow of honoring authority. That is, most Asian organizations are very hierarchical, and authority is clearly defined and defended. Subsequently, subordinates are very careful not to offend individuals in positions of higher authority or of greater age. These corporate culture values, which exist in most Asian organizations, are part of the larger value system that exists in many Asian cultures.

The Japanese Value System[2]

Although there are some commonalities, the underlying cultural values subscribed to by the Japanese are not replicated in other Asian cultures. As in other cultures, Japan's religious teachings have had a great influence on the development of its value system. For example, the Confucian influence can be observed in their emphasis on hierarchy and position, and the subtle and indirect demeanor and hidden meaning in the Japanese disposition can be traced to Zen Buddhism. A key aspect of this value system is that the Japanese view themselves as members of a group first and then as individuals. Part of the group identification involves a deeply rooted interdependence among group members and tacit obligations to the group. The ability to get along in a group environment, to adhere to the established formalities, respecting the clear class distinctions, and to behave in a conventional, predictable manner are expected. Generally, the qualities of sameness, evenness, and consistency of values and behavior dominate the culture value system of Japanese society.

Elements of this value system are reflected in the corporate culture of Japanese organizations. This pervasive corporate culture fosters norms that focus on courtesy, conformity, and caring for others within the organization. Deference based on age, rank, role, and gender are among the required behaviors of all employees. Harmony is of paramount importance. However, the suppression of women in corporate settings is a major factor that characterizes the value system of Japanese organizations. Only recently has a women's movement begun in Japan, so women managers in Japanese organizations are rare. Evidently, this value is portable. For example, only 2% of the management positions in Japanese-owned companies in the United States were held by women in 1985, a figure unchanged from 1982. Similarly, an examination of five Japanese-owned companies in the United States in 1988 found no women among 1,493 managers. Generally, though, formality, loyalty, and predictability are important attributes of the corporate value system of Japanese organizations.

The East Indian Value System[3]

Besides various tribal groups, India has a large number of ethnic communities, such as the Bengalis, Gujaritis, Sikhs, and Muslims. Each community has its own language, culture, and religion. The dominant religion is Hinduism, but there are substantial minority religions such as Islam, Sikhism, Jainism, Buddhism, Christianity, and Judaism. One indication of India's value system is that rather than attempting to assimilate these different cultures, customs, beliefs, languages, and religions into a unified whole they are accepted as they are. Despite the disparity in the culture and value systems in India, the Asian influence is apparent in the common value of respect for age and position. Also included among the values of the middle class are respect for education and competitive excellence. One of the most well known aspects of India's cultural values is the caste system, which prescribes social status at birth and offers no opportunity for upward mobility.

In East Indian organizations, the concepts of time and protocol dominate the corporate value system. Appointment schedules are not strictly adhered to, and perspectives toward work are more relaxed than in most organizations in other cultures. However, formal titles and names are almost always used, even among friends. In terms of managerial values, Indian managers at upper levels of the organization tend to underplay the use of power and are inclined to use consultative and participatory styles of management. At lower levels, however, managerial leadership tends to be paternalistic and autocratic, and power sharing with subordinates and workers is viewed as a weakness.

The Latin Value System[4]

Even though they may come from a variety of countries (e.g., Mexico, South America, Central America, and the Caribbean), individuals from these Latin cultures are drawn together by their common Spanish ancestry. Most of these countries are almost exclusively Roman Catholic, which plays a central role in their overlapping value systems. A shared value in this system is the family orientation. Family is a priority, and family obligations supersede business commitments. In most Latin cultures, men are considered superior to women. Nevertheless, women and the elderly are highly respected and cared for. Marriage and education are also shared values in Latin cultures. Marriage and education are the two primary vehicles to mobility, as they are in most other cultures. However, the social interaction among classes, which fosters an aspiration to excel in education or offer opportunities for marrying outside one's circle, are distinctly limited. As a general rule, education, good manners, and land ownership are important status symbols and indicative of one's social position. This value, social position, is of extreme significance in Latin cultures.

In Latin organizations, the value system emphasizes status and rank. Managers generally do not socialize with subordinates. However, managers are often considered part of the extended family, although their role in the family leans toward being patronizing. Subsequently, loyalty is expected and related to the personal bond between manager and subordinate. Because of the respect for managerial authority, a participative management style is not prevalent in Latin organizations—such a style would make Latin workers feel uncomfortable. Moreover, employees do not perform a task on their own—they wait out of respect for authority. Formality is important, but time and perspectives on work are very relaxed in organizations. The practice of handing out "gratuities" or bribes for getting something accomplished are legal and are an expected form of conducting business in Latin organizations. In recent years, this ethical value has begun to resemble the more restrictive values subscribed to by American organizations. Another well-known value that pervades Latin organizations is the practice of nepotism, which is expected and not considered unethical behavior.

The Eastern European Value System[5]

Because of the political-economic influence of Russia in this region, we will consider the republics of the former USSR (i.e., Russia, Ukraine, Georgia, etc.) and its satellite countries (e.g., Poland, Hungary, Bulgaria, and Czechoslovakia) as comprising this cultural cluster. People in this cluster represent over 100 nationalities, however, the five major groups are Slavs, Baltic people, people of the Caucasus, people of Soviet Central Asia, and mixed. Unlike most other cultures, where religion plays a major role in the nature of their value system, religion may play a lesser role in determining the ethical values of groups and individuals comprising this cultural cluster. Although several religions are practiced in this cluster (e.g., Islam, Buddhism, Christianity, Judaism, and Catholicism), the political climate does not promote or encourage religious activities. Generally, the people of this cluster are friendly, thoughtful, generous, and not afraid to show emotions and feelings. They are known to shake hands and state their name when meeting someone for the first time, and greetings among friends often include hugging and kisses on the cheek. Moreover, men may kiss each other on the lips or weep in public— expressions quite unique to this cultural cluster. Similar to Western cultures, individuals in this cluster are offended by untidiness and tardiness. They view punctuality as a virtue. Not so much a value as it is an idiosyncracy, a nod of the head in many countries comprising this cluster means "no" and a shake of the head means "no." Despite the absence of the religious influence, the family is the primary social unit. Moreover, there is much decorum in courting and sexual expectations between young men and women.

Since the breakup of the Soviet Union, many of the countries comprising this cluster are economically and politically volatile and still in transition. The ethical values fostered by these countries' business organizations may be just as volatile and transitory. Observers of business practices in this cluster have noted that economic and political volatility, combined with years of suppressing the development of organizations, have resulted in a pervasive Eastern European corporate value system that is significantly different from those found in organizations indigenous to Western cultures. These observers have also indicated that the corporate value system found in this cluster may be difficult for many Western managers to comprehend. The shortcomings in the system appear to be top management's inability to exert leadership in the area of espousing corporate values and the subsequent ambiguity experienced by subordinates when it comes to matters of ethical or unethical conduct in organizations.

The Western European Value System[6]

Several countries comprise this large geographical region, and many subscribe to similar cultural values. For simplicity's sake, given the many countries comprising Europe, only France and Great Britain are considered in this section.[7] As a matter of general protocol, though, individuals in western Europe tend to be rather formal and conservative. First names are never used without invitation, and that usually comes only after long association. Moreover, individuals with academic titles and degrees expect them to be used by those addressing them as a sign of respect. And, like many other cultures, punctuality is a sign of courtesy.

Generally, the religious culture of both France and Great Britain is predominantly Christian: France is primarily Roman Catholic, and Great Britain is primarily Anglican. Despite some subtle differences in their value systems, there are some commonalities as well, among them a respect for discipline and responsibility, a low tolerance for ambiguity, a view of oneself as an individual first and then as a member of a larger group, high mobility (both socially and occupationally), and esteem for education. Some differences in their value systems stem from each culture's ethnic makeup.

The ethnic population of France is a blend of Celtic, Teutonic, and Latin and includes a mixture of Nordic, Alpine, Mediterranean, a large minority of North African Arabs, and a small group of blacks from former French colonies. Because of the diverse ethnic population, most French people consider themselves members of a family first, then citizens of France, and then members of organizations. As part of greater French society, though, they share in a French culture that is well known for its flair for the arts, the graceful, and the joy of living. Another shared value common to France's diverse culture is the emphasis on tradition and *comme il faut,* or the way things are done. Also prominent in French culture is the concept of success, which is generally judged by a person's educational level, family background, and financial status rather than by direct accomplishment.

The ethnic composition of Great Britain is primarily English, Scottish, Irish, and Welsh, with sizable minorities of West Indians, East Indians, and Pakistanis. Despite the diversity of cultures, a basic sense of fair play underlies Great Britain's value system. Status is critical, and tradition and subtlety are key personal characteristics that are important in establishing status. Although the British often appear to be aloof, their demeanor is more a reflection of personal privacy and modesty along with a tendency not to register emotion in public. Generally speaking, the melding of democratic principles with a highly visible and much loved monarchy has led to a culture that is very formal and conservative yet values personal space and independence.

In European organizations, a strong concept of social order and an emphasis on rules exemplify the corporate value system. Management is formal and hierarchical, with decision-making authority concentrated at the top levels of the organization. However, many of the younger managers are moving away from the formal and hierarchical corporate value to something closer to the informal and ostensible egalitarianism more typical of the corporate value systems found in U.S. organizations.

The Australian Value System[8]

Because of its origin as a British penal colony, British cultural values are reflected in Australia's value system. A marked departure from British values is reflected in Australians' distrust of authority and rules. The Australian saying "cutting down tall poppies to size" typifies their penchant for being self-reliant and reflects their disdain for social class and money. Australians also tend to eschew formality both in social custom and in the use of titles, preferring to use first names quickly after initial introductions and formalities are over. Similar to Great Britain, a deeply ingrained sense of fair play and merit-based admiration underlie the value system of Australia. Despite this fair-play value, racial and gender discrimination are rather strong. Australia is still a male-dominated, machismo society, and immigration, especially from Asian countries, is severely restricted.

Considering their informal nature and de-emphasis on money, Australian organizations are very competitive. They consider the objective of making profits paramount and have little sympathy or respect for failure. A paradox, however, is the Australian workers' admiration for "bludgers" (i.e., those employees who can appear to be very productive but are in reality producing very little). Excessive courtesy and/or protocol in organizational settings are considered a waste of time, and friendships are not allowed to interfere with task accomplishments. Generally, the prevailing corporate value in Australian organizations is reflected in the theme "It is not how one wins but that one wins is what matters."

The American Value System[9]

Like Australia, the United States shares a common language and a common cultural heritage with Great Britain. However, many would argue that differences between America and other cultures are vast. For example, Americans are often viewed by members of other cultures as being very informal, direct, competitive, achievers, questioners, punctual, and obsessed with cleanliness. Generally, though, Americans view themselves as being caring and generous people who value their independence and entrepreneurial spirit. Most Americans, like Britons, view themselves first as individuals and then as members of a larger group. A basic sense of fair play, similar to Great Britain's, underlies the value system of America. This cultural value is reflected in the often used term "American melting pot," a concept that conveys the notion that (a) all who wish to be contributors are welcome and (b) equal opportunity exists for all who wish to try and is at the heart of the American value system. Reflected in this value is the diversity of ethnic cultures in America. From a racial-ethnic perspective, value differences among American subcultures are suggested below:

- *European American values:* individualistic, direct, rational communication, extroverted, spontaneity, casualness, egalitarian, informality
- *African American values:* camaraderie and connection with heritage, direct, informal, stylized communication, emotional expressiveness, strong community or church ties
- *Asian American values:* other-oriented, group before self, self-control, discipline, reserved, indirect communication, defined roles
- *Latino American values:* priority given to relationships, loyalty, gender roles more defined, expressive, courteous communication, spontaneous, physical closeness
- *Native American values:* oneness of all, holistic orientation, reserved communication, extended family, community oriented, privacy, noninterference

The value differences between these American subcultures suggests the concept of "ethnic culture," which can be described as the component of ethnicity that refers to that pattern of behaviors and beliefs that sets a cultural group apart from others. For women and ethnic minorities (i.e., African Americans, Asian Americans, Hispanic Americans, and Native Americans), the pattern of cultural difference is more a product of the American experience than anything else. Unlike other ethnic minorities, Hispanic Americans tend to mention the pattern of cultural differences in terms of behavioral styles, emotional expression, and personal values. With respect to values, they express an appreciation for the Hispanic American emphasis on discipline and instilling in their children a strict sense of morality. In general, they believe that Hispanic Americans are more respectful and generally have "better values" than those subscribed to by mainstream America.

Patterns of cultural differences, in terms of ethnic values, have also been evaluated using the concepts of "assimilation" and "deculturation." Under assimilation, the contention is that members of ethnic cultures adapt their behavioral patterns and norms to those of the dominant culture. With respect to women and ethnic minorities in the United States, some will adapt to the norms and values subscribed to by mainstream America. In doing so, many may camouflage their true feelings and/or suppress aspects of their own culture in public or in the presence of members of the dominant culture. Under deculturation, members of ethnic cultures retain their distinct set of norms and values with no attempt to integrate or synthesize the value system of the dominant culture. An example of deculturation is the existence of a "Chinatown" in any major American city, where there is minimal interaction between residents of Chinatown and those outside that community. Another example is the position of African Americans, who are especially sensitive to "the sacred closet of race." Often raised not to let outsiders know what their experience is like, African Americans may label as "traitors" those who reveal to members of the dominant culture their intimate feelings and experiences. As a result, many African Americans have been taught to isolate themselves and mistrust those who subscribe to dominant culture values.

▨ CULTURAL DIMENSIONS AND ETHICAL VALUES

The brief discussions of different values systems, subscribed to by diverse cultures around the world, should shed some light on how the ethical values of individuals residing in these cultures might be influenced. However, the various dimensions comprising each value system (e.g., customs, religion, law, respect for individuality, national identity and loyalty, and the rights of property) make it difficult to assess the deontological norms of individuals from different cultures in organizational settings. Fortunately, a typology derived from Geert Hofstede's (1980) research has made such an assessment possible.

One conclusion drawn from Hofstede's research is that societies differ along four major cultural dimensions:

- *Power distance*—the degree to which a society accepts inequalities in organizational relationships
- *Uncertainty avoidance*—the degree to which individuals in a society feel threatened by situations that are unstructured, unclear, or unpredictable
- *Individualism/collectivism*—the extent to which individuals in a society view themselves as individuals or part of a larger group
- *Masculinity/femininity*—the extent to which a society's dominant values emphasize assertiveness and materialism versus concern for people and quality of life

Table 3.1 indicates where the various cultures discussed in this chapter fall on each of these dimensions. The numerical values show how countries differ on each dimension. For example, the power distance score is 81 for Mexico and 13 for Israel. This is interpreted to mean that Mexicans generally accept inequalities in their relationships, whereas Israelis do not. The other scores in

Table 3.1. Differences Among Cultures Along Four Dimensions

Country/Culture	Cultural Dimensions			
	Power Distance	Uncertainty Avoidance	Individualism	Masculinity
Argentina	49	86	46	56
Australia	36	51	90	61
Brazil	69	76	38	49
Canada	39	48	80	52
Denmark	18	23	74	16
France	68	86	71	43
Germany (E.R.)	35	65	67	66
Great Britain	35	35	89	66
Indonesia	78	48	14	46
India	77	40	48	56
Israel	13	81	54	47
Japan	54	92	46	95
Mexico	81	82	30	69
Netherlands	38	53	80	14
Panama	95	86	11	44
Spain	57	86	51	42
Sweden	31	29	71	5
Thailand	64	64	20	34
Turkey	66	85	37	45
United States	40	46	91	62

SOURCE: Adapted from Hofstede (1980).

this table are interpreted similarly. Tables 3.2, 3.3, 3.4, and 3.5 list several characteristics associated with each of these four cultural dimensions. Some of the ethical implications associated with these dimensions and their characteristics are highlighted in the following discussions.

Power Distance

The characteristics listed in Table 3.2 provide a fairly comprehensive assessment of subordinate-superior relationships in cultures where there are high or low levels of power distance. The concept of power distance has been

Table 3.2. Power Distance Characteristics in Organizations

Low Power Distance Cultures	High Power Distance Cultures
1. Employees are less afraid to disagree with their managers	1. Employees fear disagreeing with their managers
2. Employees are more cooperative	2. Employees reluctant to trust each other
3. Higher-educated employees hold much less authoritarian values than lower-educated ones	3. Higher- and lower-educated employees show similar values about authority
4. Mixed feeling about employees' participation in management	4. Ideological support for employees' participation in management
5. Close supervision negatively evaluated by subordinates	5. Close supervision positively evaluated by subordinates
6. Stronger perceived work ethic among employees	6. Weaker perceived work ethic among employees
7. Managers more satisfied with participative superior	7. Managers more satisfied with directive or persuasive superior
8. More consideration among managers	8. Less consideration among managers
9. Subordinates' preference for managers' decision-making style clearly centered on consultative, give-and-take style	9. Subordinates' preference for managers' decision-making style polarized between autocratic-paternalistic and majority rule

SOURCE: Adapted from Hofstede (1984, p. 92).

incorporated in ethical research in different ways. In one research study, this concept was assessed within the context of differential association theory (Ferrell, Zey-Ferrell, & Krugman, 1983). Essentially, this theory assumes that ethical/unethical behavior in organizations is learned through the process of interacting with peers rather than with superiors. Applications of this theory have revealed that differential associations with peers are the strongest predictor of ethical/unethical behavior in organizations. One practical implication stemming from results of the applications is that, in cultures where the degree of power distance is low or moderate, individuals look more to their peers than to their superiors for guidance in terms of ethical conduct.

Uncertainty Avoidance

The ambiguity that individuals from different cultures might experience in organizations is captured by the uncertainty avoidance characteristics listed in Table 3.3. A major implication of these characteristics is that when individu-

Table 3.3. Uncertainty Avoidance Characteristic in Organizations

Low Uncertainty Avoidance Cultures	High Uncertainty Avoidance Cultures
1. Employee optimism about motives behind company activities	1. Employee pessimism about motives behind company activities
2. Company rules may be broken for pragmatic reasons	2. Company rules should not be broken for any reason
3. Loyalty to employer is not seen as a virtue	3. Loyalty to employer is seen as a virtue
4. Lower average age in higher level jobs	4. Higher average age in higher level jobs
5. Stronger achievement motivation	5. Weaker achievement motivation
6. Competition between employees can be fair and right	6. Competition between employees is emotionally disapproved of
7. Acceptance of foreigners as managers	7. Suspicion toward foreigners as managers
8. More employee risk taking	8. Less employee risk taking
9. Hope of success among employees	9. Fear of failure among employees

SOURCE: Adapted from Hofstede (1984, pp. 132-133).

als from cultures where the level of uncertainty avoidance is low enter an organization, the absence of formalized standards and codes of conduct may cause them to perceive the acceptability of the organization's various activities and procedures (ethical or unethical) as ambiguous. Thus individuals from such cultures may sometimes accept unethical behavior, especially where there is no formal standard or rule to guide their behavior (Ferrell & Skinner, 1988). It has been suggested that individuals from high uncertainty avoidance cultures are more likely than those from low uncertainty avoidance cultures to consider organizational codes of ethics when forming their own deontological norms (Vitell, Nwachukwu, & Barnes, 1993).

Individualism/Collectivism

Moral involvement with the organization they work for is one characteristic that typifies individuals from collectivist cultures (refer to Table 3.4). Because these individuals cannot easily distance themselves from the larger group of which they are a member (i.e., the organization), they will most likely be influenced by the norms of the group. Therefore, the existence of ethical codes is likely to exact compliance from such individuals. However, employees from individualist cultures, who may be more concerned with their own

Table 3.4. Individualism/Collectivism Characteristics in Organizations

Individualistic Cultures	Collectivist Cultures
1. Employees are emotionally independent from the company	1. Employees are emotionally dependent on the company
2. More importance attached to freedom and challenge in jobs	2. More importance attached to training and use of skills in jobs
3. Managers aspire to leadership	3. Managers aspire to conformity
4. Managers rate having autonomy as being more important	4. Managers rate having security as being more important
5. Individual decisions are considered better than group decisions	5. Group decisions are considered better than individual decisions
6. Managers choose pleasure, affection, and security as life goals	6. Managers choose duty, expertness, and prestige as life goals
7. Employee initiative is encouraged	7. Employee initiative is frowned upon
8. Fewer years of schooling needed to do a given job	8. More years of schooling needed to do a given job
9. Employees attracted to small companies	9. Employees attracted to large companies

SOURCE: Adapted from Hofstede (1984, p. 166).

self-interest, will tend to be influenced less by organizational codes of ethics (Robin & Reidenbach, 1987). Studies have shown that ethical/unethical behavior in organizations is sometimes determined by the extent to which individuals consider the group (i.e., the organization) as being more important than themselves, or vice versa (Hegarty & Sims, 1979).

Masculinity/Femininity

Characteristics comprising this dimension (see Table 3.5) suggest that there are some cultural environments that are more conducive to unethical behavior than others. The focus on materialism in some masculine cultures, for instance, may contribute significantly to an individual's engagement in unethical behavior. Practices such as high-pressure sales tactics may be viewed as simply good business in some masculine cultures but may be considered unethical in more feminine cultures. In masculine cultures, individuals may not view certain work-related activities as having an ethical component because such activities are not defined by their culture as involving ethics. Consequently, individuals from highly masculine cultures may be less likely than those from highly feminine cultures to be influenced by organizational codes of ethics.

Table 3.5. Masculine/Feminine Characteristics in Organizations

Masculine Cultures	Feminine Cultures
1. Greater value differences between men and women in the same jobs	1. Smaller or no value differences between men and women in the same jobs
2. Managers less attracted to service role	2. Managers have more of a service ideal
3. Achievement defined in terms of recognition and wealth	3. Achievement defined in terms of human contacts and living environment
4. Greater work centrality	4. Work less central in people's lives
5. Company's interference in private life is accepted	5. Company's interference in private life is rejected
6. Employees prefer more salary to shorter working hours	6. Employees prefer shorter working hours to more salary
7. Stronger achievement motivation among employees	7. Weaker achievement motivation among employees
8. Managers more interested in leadership, independence, and self-realization	8. Managers less interested in leadership, independence, and self-realization
9. Earnings, recognition, advancement, and challenge relatively more important	9. Relationship with manager, cooperation, friendly work environment, and employment security more important

SOURCE: Adapted from Hofstede (1984, pp. 166-167).

Generally, the characteristics listed in Tables 3.2 through 3.5 suggest that as societies differ with regards to these cultural dimensions so will the various components of their ethical paradigms. These characteristics also suggest how all four of the cultural dimensions relate to ethics in the sense that they may influence the individual's perception of ethical situations, norms for ethical behavior, and ethical judgments, among other factors. They also hold implications for managing ethics in organizations where there are high levels of cultural and human diversity.

Synthesizing Culture and Ethics

A more extensive list of cultural clusters, together with sample countries comprising each cluster, is shown in Table 3.6. When combined with Hofstede's (1980) typology of cultural dimensions and their associated characteristics, a practical framework for considering the potential impact of increasing diversity on organizational ethics can be derived. Such a framework is presented in

Table 3.6. Different Cultural Clusters

Cluster	Sample Countries Comprising Cluster
Anglo-American	United States, Canada, Australia, New Zealand, United Kingdom, Ireland South Africa
Latin European	France, Belgium, Italy, Portugal, Spain
Latin American	Argentina, Venezuela, Chile, Mexico, Peru, Colombia
Far Eastern	Malaysia, Hong Kong, China, Singapore, Philippines, Vietnam, Indonesia, Taiwan, Thailand
Arab	Abu-Dhabi, Oman, Bahrain, United Arab Emirates, Kuwait, Saudi Arabia
Near Eastern	Turkey, Iran, Greece
Nordic	Finland, Norway, Denmark, Sweden
Germanic	Austria, Germany, Switzerland
Independent	Brazil, Japan, India, Israel

SOURCE: Based on Hofstede (1980).

Table 3.7. As individuals from diverse cultures continue to immigrate to the United States and become members of U.S. organizations, frameworks such as this one will offer managers a potential tool for aiding the development of strategies and models for managing ethics in organizations.

Specifically, the framework presented in Table 3.7 allows organizations to determine where each cultural group/individual in their workforce, who may be from one of the cultural clusters, falls on each cultural dimension (i.e., low, moderate, or high). Once this determination is made, an assessment of each group's/individual's deontological ethical norms can be made, the results of which should give the organization some idea of the direction and magnitude of any impact that increasing diversity might potentially have on its existing ethics paradigm.

Despite the appeal of such a framework, caution is urged in its application. The framework is based on the notion that countries comprising a particular cultural cluster are more similar on several dimensions of culture than countries comprising another cultural cluster. However, the culture of individual countries within a cluster may differ on several cultural dimensions. These differences must be considered when using such a framework to assess the

Table 3.7. Cultural Clusters and Dimensions

Cultural Cluster	Cultural Dimension			
	Individualism[a]	Power Distance	Uncertainty Avoidance	Masculinity[b]
Anglo-American	High	Low/Moderate	Low	High
Germanic	Moderate	Low	Moderate/High	Moderate/High
Nordic	Moderate/High	Low	Low/Moderate	Low
Near Eastern	Low	High	High	Moderate
Arab	Low	High	Moderate/High	Moderate
Far Eastern	Low	High	Low/Moderate	Moderate
Latin American	Low	High	High	High
Latin European	High	High	High	High

SOURCE: Based on Hofstede (1980).
a. Low individualism is equivalent to collectivism.
b. Low masculinity is equivalent to femininity.

deontological norms of groups and individuals who may come from a particular cultural cluster.

Issues to Consider

Research studies cited in this chapter clearly indicate that both individual and organizational ethics are influenced by cultural value systems. These studies also suggest that the value system of a given culture determines the nature of the ethical paradigm subscribed to by groups and individuals residing in that culture. As demonstrated in this chapter, values and thus ethics may vary substantially among the different groups comprising U.S. organizations. At issue is whether, or to what extent, the paradigms will undergo a shift as these groups and individuals take up residence in a culture that subscribes to a different set of ethical paradigms. Also at issue is whether, or to what extent, the paradigms that these groups and individuals bring with them will cause a shift in the ethical paradigms of their host culture. These issues are addressed in Chapter 4, where the emphasis is on possible paradigm shifts in organizational ethics as groups and individuals from different racial, ethnic, cultural, and otherwise diverse backgrounds become organizational participants.

◩ NOTES

1. Sources of information for this section include Steward, Cheung, and Yeung (1992) and Andrew (1988).

2. Sources of information for this section include Ratio and Rodgers (1984), Goodman (1990a), Orr (1993), and Sen (1993).

3. Sources of information for this section include Singh (1993), Sinha (1992), Lee and Tefft (1989), Jain (1991), and Singh and Hofstede (1990).

4. Sources of information for this section include Gutierrez (1993), Gomez (1993), Radebaugh (1976), and Thiederman (1991).

5. Sources of information for this section include Bose (1993), Hertz (1991), Nicholls (1992), and Axtell (1985).

6. Sources of information for this section include Sen (1993), Goodman (1990b), and McLaughlin (1990).

7. An acknowledgment is made here that the cultures of France and Great Britain are not necessarily representative of other cultures in Western Europe. However, their influence in this region has resulted in some similar cultural attributes among countries comprising this cultural cluster.

8. Sources of information for this section include Kramer (1993), Malic, Rees, Johnstone, Chang, and Knowles (1992), Kasper (1992), and Elton (1992).

9. Sources of information for this section include Hofstede (1980), Keefe (1992), Tung (1993), Piturro and Mahoney (1991), and Bennett (1986).

4

Ethical Values and
Diversity in Organizations

When an organization recruits individuals from diverse cultures, the individuals may bring varying ideals of what is right and what is wrong to the workplace. Consequently, there is a possibility that the ethical values subscribed to by the organization will undergo transformation.

Discussions provided in Chapter 3 suggested that relationships exist not only between cultural value systems and the personal values of groups and individuals but also between cultural value systems and the ethical values of organizations. The model shown in Figure 4.1 depicts these relationships. This model indicates that the cultural value system of a particular culture influences the ethical values of groups and individuals residing in the culture, and the ethical values of organizations operating in the culture, as well as the corporate codes of ethics that these organizations might have. The model also shows that three ethics paradigms exist simultaneously in organizations: the corporate code of ethics, the corporate culture, and the ethical values of groups and individuals employed by organizations.

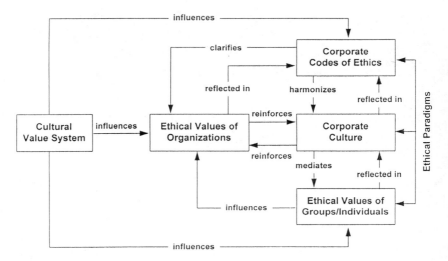

Figure 4.1. Relationship Between Cultural Values and Organizational Ethics

As shown, the ethical values of groups and individuals are reflected in organizations' corporate culture, and corporate culture is reflected in organizations' codes of ethics. In turn, organizations' codes of ethics clarify the ethical values of organizations and harmonize their corporate culture, and corporate culture mediates the ethical values of groups and individuals comprising organizations. Finally, the ethical values of groups and individuals influence the ethical values of organizations, which are reflected in the corporate codes of ethics, and corporate culture and the ethical values of organizations mutually influence one another. Besides depicting the interrelationship among these various ethics-related factors, the model suggests that the ethical paradigms existing in organizations, particularly corporate culture and corporates codes of ethics, are susceptible to change as conditions within the relationships undergo change.

The fact that these paradigms are interrelated to varying degrees resurfaces the issue of their potentially being transmogrified by increasing diversity in the workplace. A major question we seek to answer in this chapter is how might an organization's ethics paradigm (i.e., corporate culture and thus corporate codes of ethics) be affected as the workplace becomes more diverse? A possible answer to this question is given in the form of conceptual models, which are presented later in this chapter. Specifically, the models postulate about the shifts that the corporate codes of ethics and the corporate culture paradigms will potentially undergo as a result of increasing diversity. Discussions of these two paradigms precede presentation of the models.

◩ CORPORATE CULTURE AND ETHICS

Together with the definition given in Chapter 1, corporate culture has been described as

> a general constellation of beliefs, mores, customs, value systems, behavioral norms, and ways of doing business that are unique to each corporation, that set a pattern for corporate activities and actions, and that describe the implicit and emergent patterns of behavioral and emotions characterizing life in the organization. (Tunstall, 1983, p. 15)

The various components of corporate culture (e.g., norms, customs, beliefs, standards, and values) denote as well as connote its intricate relationship to the ethical system that exists within organizations.

Indeed, research has shown that corporate culture can have a profound impact on the ethical standards and moral practices of individuals in organizations (Akers, 1989). Results of such research have encouraged organizations to undertake the task of managing corporate culture, with the goal of promoting a high standard of ethical conduct among organizational members (Fisse & Braithwaite, 1983). The prevailing sentiment among organizations is that the creation of a unitary, cohesive corporate culture around a set of core moral values is the solution to enhancing ethical behavior (Sinclair, 1993). Theoretically, then, an effective corporate culture should encourage ethical behavior and discourage unethical behavior. However, attempts to use corporate culture to encourage ethical behavior often fail.

Regulating Ethics
Through Corporate Culture

In 1990, AT&T implemented a program of corporate culture change. During the change process, top management explicitly articulated the organization's value system to employees. Training was given to employees to reshape their norms and modify their behavior in support of the organization's ethical values. As a means of maintaining the integrity of the cultural change, recruitment efforts targeted only those potential employees whose personal values and ethics were consistent with AT&T's value system (Buchowicz, 1990; Petty & Cacioppo, 1990).

Despite the tremendous effort to encourage ethical behavior and discourage unethical behavior through corporate culture change, the effort fell short of its goal; in 1995, an AT&T executive and 16 others were implicated in an insider trading scam (Kalish, 1995). Participants in this unethical behavior allegedly used information, supplied by the mid-level executive in AT&T's human resources department, to trade on the stock of potential AT&T acquisition targets over a four-year period. This type of unethical behavior on the part of AT&T employees is hardly unique, many other organizations have had similar experiences. Such experiences support the claims of those who doubt that organizations are able to, or should, regulate ethical behavior through their corporate culture.

Effectiveness of Corporate Culture

The AT&T experience brings up the issue of whether the ethical values disseminated through corporate culture are enduring or whether they are susceptible to alteration by the values of those who are subject to its influence, especially newcomers to the organization. Let's first examine this issue within the context of society at large. According to classical assimilationist theory, the best option for newcomers to a given society is to shed their ethnicity as quickly as possible. Most, however, choose among these nonexclusive options:

1. Assimilate the mainstream's cultural values
2. Assimilate a particular minority's or subculture's values
3. Preserve their own cultural values.

In a recent study (Schauffler, 1994), it was found that 48% of the Vietnamese responding to a survey consider themselves "Vietnamese" as opposed to "Vietnamese American," "Asian," or "American" (Option 3). In contrast, 48% of the Haitians responding to the same survey consider themselves "Haitian Americans" (Option 1); 42% of the Nicaraguans responding to the survey consider themselves "Latino" or "Hispanic" (Option 2). A major finding of the study was that, no matter what option is chosen, during the assimilation process the values of both the newcomers and the host society undergo transformation.

Within the context of organizations, the issue becomes whether corporate culture erases or at least diminishes national or societal cultural characteristics and whether (or to what extent) individuals from diverse cultures are able to transform corporate culture. According to research conducted by André Laurent (1983), the answer to the first issue is no. His research revealed that employees and managers bring their race, ethnicity, and cultural values to the workplace.

He contends that many managers assume that employees working for the same organization, even if they are from different racial, ethnic, and cultural backgrounds, are more similar than different. In reality, though, employees adopt what has been called "reactive ethnic identity." That is, they maintain and even strengthen their racial, ethnic, and cultural differences in organizations. Moreover, Laurent contends that even though organizations are becoming more similar, employees' behavior maintains a racial, ethnic, and cultural uniqueness. One reason given by Laurent for this "reactive ethnic identity" phenomenon is the pressure to conform to corporate culture.

The message conveyed here is that attempts to manage ethical behavior through corporate culture may bring out resistance from employees who subscribe to different ethical paradigms, causing them to cling more firmly to their own racial, ethnic, cultural, or subculture values. Ethicists (e.g., Buller, Kohls, & Anderson, 1991) have argued that likely carriers of ethical values are individuals from diverse racial, ethnic, and cultural backgrounds. Intentionally or not, behaviors that reflect the values and beliefs of their culture will predominate in both those individuals and the organization. Ultimately, will these behaviors lead to a transmogrification of corporate culture, or a shift in this ethical paradigm? The conceptual models presented later in this chapter will help provide an answer to this question.

▨ ETHICAL CODES IN ORGANIZATIONS

The results of ethics-related research (cf. Business Roundtable, 1988; Hoffman, 1989; Touche-Ross Foundation, 1988) indicate that U.S. organizations are increasingly employing codes of conduct for encouraging ethical behavior on the part of their employees. According to Bennett (1988), these written codes of ethics usually deal with topics such as conflicts of interest, confidentiality of corporate information, misappropriation of assets, bribes, kickbacks, and political contributions.

In his study of 281 firms, Chatov (1980) noted the percentage of these firms that included prohibitive behavior such as those in their code of ethics. The types of prohibitive behaviors and the percentage of firms listing them in their code of ethics included the following: extortion, gifts, kickbacks (76%), conflict of interest (65%), illegal political payments (59%), violation of laws in general (57%), use of insider information (43%), bribery (37%), falsification of corporate accounts (28%), violation of antitrust laws (25%), moonlighting (25%), illegal payments abroad (23%), revealing company secrets (22%), ignorance of work-related laws (22%), and fraud and deception (11%).

A survey of 2,000 managers revealed that more than 60% believe that a code of ethics containing the prohibitions in this list raises the level of ethics in organizations (Holmquist, 1993). Reasons given for these beliefs are that codes of ethics serve merely as guidelines for those who already possess a basic moral sense and as devices for helping them clarify their own ethical values and standards. In some instances, that is, individuals do not know what is ethical. So besides serving as a crutch for those who may need a little extra moral strength to bolster their position, corporate codes of ethics are viewed by them as being very helpful in understanding and guiding their everyday ethical actions.

Effectiveness of Corporate Codes

Whereas some see value in codes of ethics, others are skeptical that any kind of written code can mediate ethical conduct. They point out that even respected companies like General Electric, which have written codes of ethics, are not immune from major scandals (cf. Murphy, 1988). Moreover, they perceive such codes as devices that "deresponsibilize" individuals. They contend that individuals do not have to think—they just apply the written codes of conduct they have learned and which, through training, have programmed them to respond in a certain "corporate way" (cf. de Bettignies, 1991). An assumption made here, of course, is that organizations offer training (either formal or informal) in ethics.

The results of one study (Posner & Schmidt, 1992) found that more than 75% of the respondents reported that their organization did not offer ethics workshops. Evidently, the popular view held by these organizations is that the presence of an ethics code is enough to promote ethical behavior and that ethics workshops are redundant. Generally, though, those who are skeptical of corporate codes of ethics consider them ineffective because (a) organizations that adopt ethical codes do not back them up with appropriate support structures (e.g., ethical workshops and leadership) and (b) ethical conduct can only be determined by each individual's personal code of conduct (cf. McCuddy, Reichardt, & Schroeder, 1993; Pettit et al., 1990).

Ethical Codes and Diversity

It has been argued that although individuals from different backgrounds can have the same moral values they may behave differently when faced with a common situation because of the reasoning process through which they apply codes of ethics (Stoner & Freeman, 1989; Wines & Napier, 1989). Conversely, it has been argued that individuals with different moral values and ethical codes may agree on the appropriate behavior in a particular situation but not on the moral values or ethical codes underlying the behaviors (Buller et al., 1991).

The message conveyed here is that as organizations become more diverse they will likely face dilemmas of split loyalties (on the part of employees) with respect to corporate codes of ethics. An issue raised is whether, or to what extent, individuals from diverse racial, ethnic, cultural, and otherwise diverse backgrounds will or should capitulate their personal ethical code to the organization's written ethical code, especially when they may resent having notions of right and wrong boiled down to a list of behaviors that are prohibited by the organization.

▧ THE NATURE OF ETHICAL PARADIGMS

In an earlier section of this chapter, it was noted that whether individuals from diverse cultures choose to assimilate the host society's values, assimilate the values of a subculture or minority culture within the society, or retain their own values, the values of the host society will be affected to some degree. What this clearly suggests is that the ethics paradigms of a given culture are susceptible to the influence of ethics paradigms brought into the culture by others. However, if the ethical values subscribed to by American organizations were to enter into a paradigmatic shift, due to increases in workforce diversity, the reason may be attributed more to Americans' willingness to accept the ethical standards of diverse cultures than to the intentional or unintentional efforts exerted by those with different or opposing ethical paradigms. Rushworth Kidder (1992), former senior columnist of the *Christian Science Monitor,* supports this view in the following statement:

> In the nineteenth century, one of the highest goals of Western nations was a sense of standards. We took our standards out into the rest of the world, colonized other regions, and imposed those standards. Were we tolerant of what we found there? Not at all. If the people whom we were trying to "civilize" didn't want to get "civilized," we went out and "civilized" them anyway! At the end of a gun, or however we had to do it, but we civilized them. Why? To bring them up to our standards. By the 1960s, this attitude had shifted 180 degrees. Tolerance was what mattered most. As long as somebody said, "Yes, this is what I stand for, this is what I want to do," one was expected to be wholly tolerant of any conceivable value structure. (p. 12)

One might conclude from this statement that although Americans do not necessarily "sell out" their values to those who may challenge them they have become more sensitive to, and more willing to accept, the values of others—even though those values may verge on the immoral by American standards. Judging from the tenor of this statement, the general sentiment of Americans appears to be "Don't judge the values of others, when different from ours, as necessarily immoral; find ways to operate from their ethical points of view, and do not demand that they operate only by our ground rules." Similar sentiments appear to exist among American managers.

Posner and Schmidt (1992) found, for instance, that although the values of American managers are enduring they are also sensitive to social trends (e.g., diversity). Exemplifying this sensitivity is the management at Johnson & Johnson. It has been noted that newly hired employees, from diverse backgrounds, are challenged to explore the validity of the ethical codes subscribed to by the company (Byrne, 1988). Because a code of ethics is one of the main paradigms through which the values of an organization are acted out and thus should reflect the values of those subjected to it, the implication is that diverse employees are given an opportunity to influence ethical standards at Johnson & Johnson.

The main point conveyed in this section is that the ethics paradigms subscribed to by U.S. organizations are susceptible to being influenced by the ethical values brought to the workplace by individuals from diverse racial, ethnic, cultural, and otherwise diverse backgrounds. Although it has been argued that to challenge the behavior that arises from a particular ethical value is appropriate but to challenge the ethical value itself is inappropriate, indications are that the ethical values of U.S. organizations are being challenged as they become more diverse. As these organizations become more diverse, the challenge is likely to come from those diverse individuals and groups who may feel that their values are not being reflected in existing organizational paradigms. In the next few sections of this chapter, discussions focus on conceptual models. Propositions are derived from the models about shifts that are likely to occur in organizational ethics paradigms as a result of increasing diversity.

Paradigm Shifts in Organizations

In Chapter 1, an ethics-diversity process model was presented. The process by which increasing diversity in the workplace affects ethics paradigms in organizations was suggested in this model. Essentially, the model proposed that increasing diversity in an organization's workforce creates greater communication style and value differences. These differences proposedly affect the organization's cultural network (i.e., the mechanism that teaches and enforces the ethical values subscribed to by the organization), which, in turn, stabilizes the organization's corporate culture. Finally, the organization's corporate culture influences the organizational ethics paradigm—namely, corporate codes of ethics.

Also in Chapter 1, the following question was posed: If there is a shift in the ethics paradigms subscribed to by organizations, attributable to increasing diversity, what will be the nature of this shift? In response to this question, it is proposed in this book that the nature of such shifts is based on elements comprising the ethics-diversity process model (e.g., communication differences, value conflicts, and the cultural network) and two additional factors: the current level of diversity in an organization's workforce and the rate at which the organization's workforce becomes more diverse.

With respect to the first factor, an assumption made is that the organization has a history of having either a low or a high proportion of racially,

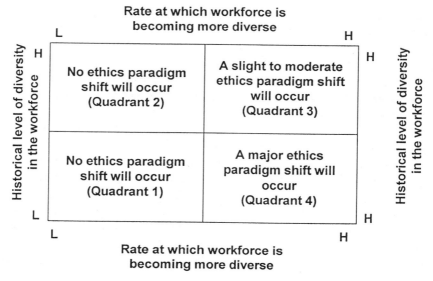

Figure 4.2. Propositions That Diversity Will Lead to Ethics Paradigm Shift

ethnically, culturally, and otherwise diverse employees in its workforce. With respect to the second factor, the rate at which racially, ethnically, culturally, and otherwise diverse individuals are added to an organization's workforce can also be high or low. When the rate is high, its workforce becomes significantly more diverse over a relatively short period of time. When the rate is low, its workforce gradually becomes more diverse over a relatively longer period of time. By combining these discrete dimensions (i.e., high or low rate at which an organization's workforce becomes more diverse and a currently high or low proportion of diverse employees in the workforce), the conceptual model presented in Figure 4.2 is derived.

No Ethics Paradigm Shift

Quadrant 1 of the model relates to the type of organization where the level of diversity in its workforce has a history of being low and the rate at which its workforce is becoming more diverse is low. In this type of organization, increases in diversity are expected to occur gradually in small increments over a relatively long period of time. Because only a few culturally, ethnically, racially, and otherwise diverse individuals are gradually added to the organization's workforce, communication problems and value conflicts are minimized. Subsequently, the organization's cultural network will be relatively unaffected, thus maintaining the type of corporate culture that is able to effectively communicate, teach, and enforce ethical values and standards.

This quadrant would be most relevant to organizations operating in states such as Vermont, New Hamphire, and Maine, where there are very few ethnic minorities and foreign nationals in these states' population and thus very little diversity in their workforce. The historical level of diversity in these organizations' workforce can be considered low. Also, only a few hundred ethnic minorities and foreign nationals are moving into these states annually ("Where the New Wave," 1991). Subsequently, the rate at which the workforce of these organizations is becoming more diverse is also low. With such a small number of diverse individuals gradually being integrated into a predominately mainstream American value system and corporate culture, there is little chance that the ethical values brought to the workplace by these individuals will cause a shift in these organizations' ethics paradigms.

Quadrant 2 of the model relates to the type of organization where the level of diversity in its workforce has a history of being high and the rate at which its workforce is becoming more diverse is low. Because the level of diversity has a history of being high, the organization's cultural network is adept at accommodating different communication styles and has mechanisms (e.g., socialization processes) in place to reconcile value conflicts. Subsequently, the small number of diverse individuals gradually added to the organization's workforce over a relatively long period of time can easily be integrated into the workforce without disrupting the organization's cultural network or destabilizing its corporate culture.

General Electric (GE) Corporation might fit into this quadrant. This company has maintained a highly diverse workforce over the years. Management at GE also has instituted successful, ongoing training programs designed to rapidly socialize new employees into the company's corporate culture (Garvin, 1993). As GE's workforce has slowly become more diverse over time, these programs have ensured that communication and value differences attributable to diversity increases have had a minimum impact on the company's culture network. As a result, GE has maintained a stable corporate culture, which has prevented any material shift in its ethics paradigm.

It is proposed, then, that when the level of diversity in an organization's workforce has a history of being either high or low and the rate at which its

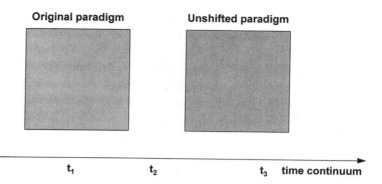

t₁: Nature of paradigm with low or high level of diversity in work force
t₂: Workforce becomes more diverse at a low rate
t₃: Nature of paradigm after diversity level in workforce increases at a low rate

Figure 4.3. No Shift in Organization's Ethics Paradigm

workforce becomes more diverse is low, there will be no shift in the organization's existing ethics paradigm. This proposition is shown pictorially in Figure 4.3. The organization's original ethics paradigm is represented by the shaded square at Time t_1. After the organization's workforce begins to become more diverse at a slow rate at Time t_2, its ethics paradigm remains essentially the same at Time t_3.

Slight to Moderate Ethics Paradigm Shift

Quadrant 3 of the model shown in Figure 4.2 relates to the type of organization where the level of diversity in its workforce has a history of being high and the rate at which its workforce is becoming more diverse is high (i.e., diverse individuals and groups are expected to be added to the organization's workforce rapidly and in large numbers over a relatively short period of time). Because the level of diversity in its workforce has a history of being high, the organization's cultural network is adept at accommodating different communication styles and has mechanisms in place to reconcile value conflicts.

However, it is proposed in this book that the sheer magnitude and high rate of speed at which diverse individuals and groups are added to the organization's workforce will create barriers to the effective functioning of the organization's cultural network, resulting in slight to moderate disruptions in its corporate culture. The disruptions will proposedly destabilize the organization's corporate culture to the extent that it is restricted, but not prohibited, in its ability to transmit and enforce ethical standards.

Based on this author's personal knowledge of the operations at Hewlett-Packard's San Diego, California facility, this company would fit into this quadrant. Although diversity in the workforce at this facility has historically been high, a greater commitment to diversity resulted in a rapid increase in the number of minority employees (e.g., blacks, Mexicans, Indochinese, and Filipinos). A destabilization in the corporate culture at this facility was evident for months following the increase in diversity.

However, because of its prior experience with diversity, the facility's destabilization of corporate culture was minimized. Even though management knew how to respond (e.g., intensified training programs) to minimize the disruption, concessions still had to be made to restore stability to the corporate culture. For example, minor (and some major) ethical infractions committed by new (minority) employees were overlooked when sanctions would have been assessed prior to the increase in diversity. As a way of accommodating a more highly diverse workforce, management revised certain policies that relaxed some behaviors that were previously considered borderline unethical.

It is proposed, then, that when the level of diversity in an organization's workforce has a history of being high and the rate at which its workforce becomes more diverse is high, there will be a slight to moderate shift in the organization's original ethics paradigm. This proposition is shown pictorially in Figure 4.4. Again, the organization's original ethics paradigm is represented by the shaded square at Time t_1. At Time t_2, the organization's workforce begins to become more diverse at a high rate. Because the organization's corporate culture is restricted in its ability to effectively transmit and enforce ethical standards, due to the impact of communication problems and value conflicts, it becomes susceptible to the influences of the different ethical paradigms brought to the workplace by diverse individuals and groups.

Eventually, the organizational response is to make slight to moderate adjustments in its ethical standards to accommodate ethical diversity in its workforce. This response represents a slight to moderate shift in the organization's original ethics paradigm. What remains of the organization's original ethics paradigm is represented by the shaded area (A) at Time t_3. Although it has undergone a shift, the shaded area (A) indicates that the organization's ethics paradigm has retained most of its original content. Point B, at Time t_3,

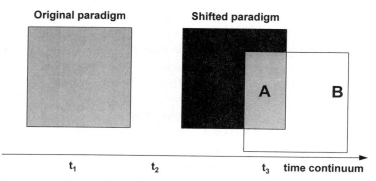

t₁: Nature of paradigm with low level of diversity in workforce
t₂: Workforce becomes more diverse at a high rate
t₃: Nature of paradigm after diversity level in workforce increases at a high rate
A = Remnant of original paradigm
B = Shifted portion of paradigm that has incorporated most of the diverse moral values in a highly diverse workforce

Figure 4.4. Slight to Moderate Shift in Organization's Ethics Paradigm

represents the shifted portion of the organization's original ethics paradigm that has incorporated some of the diverse ethical and moral values in its highly diverse workforce.

Major Ethics Paradigm Shift

Finally, Quadrant 4 of the model relates to the type of organization where the level of diversity in its workforce has a history of being low and the rate at which its workforce is becoming more diverse is high. Because the level of diversity in its workforce has a history of being low, such an organization has very little or no experience with diversity. Subsequently, this type of organization will probably have no mechanisms in place to help overcome the communication problems and value conflicts created by the rapid addition of a large number of diverse individuals and groups to its workforce.

Consequently, manifold ethnic, cultural, racial, attitudinal, and behavioral differences will likely generate a multitude of communication problems and value conflicts that will cause a major malfunctioning of the organization's cultural network. It is proposed here that this malfunctioning will result in a highly unstable corporate culture that will not only be unable to effectively transmit and enforce the organization's ethical values, but its core values will be highly susceptible to alterations or supplantation by the ethical and moral values brought to the workplace by diverse individuals and groups.

The experience of Racal-Vadic, a U.S. manufacturer of computer modems, would qualify this company to fit into this quadrant. The diversity level of this company's workforce has historically been low. In a provocative move to ensure a highly qualified workforce, the company added a significant number of technically trained, foreign immigrants to its workforce. Although these employees brought a tremendous amount of knowledge and technical expertise to the workplace, as their representation increased in the company's workforce so did instances of communication and value conflict (Buonocore, 1992).

Because of the lack of experience with diversity and the rapid rate at which diversity levels increased, the company had no mechanisms in place to reconcile the communications problems and value conflicts. Only after several years of training programs and further increases in the level of diversity was corporate culture stabilized. By this time, however, the workforce consisted mainly of foreign nationals and the core values of the company had changed—and so had the company's ethics paradigms.

It is proposed, then, that when the level of diversity in an organization's workforce has a history of being low and the rate at which its workforce becomes more diverse is high, there will be a major shift in the organization's existing ethics paradigm. This proposition is shown pictorially in Figure 4.5. In this figure, the organization's original ethics paradigm is represented by the shaded square at Time t_1. At Time t_2, the organization's workforce begins to become more diverse at a high rate. The severe disruption to the organization's corporate culture, due to the absence of mechanisms designed to help overcome communication problems and value conflicts, renders it virtually incapable of effectively transmitting and enforcing ethical standards. In its unstable state, the different ethical and moral values brought to the workplace by diverse individuals and groups begin to alter and, in some cases, supplant the organization's core ethical values. Eventually, a major shift occurs in the organization's original ethics paradigm.

What remains of the organization's original ethics paradigm is represented by the shaded area (A) at Time t_3. This shaded area indicates that the different ethical paradigms brought to the workplace by diverse individuals and groups

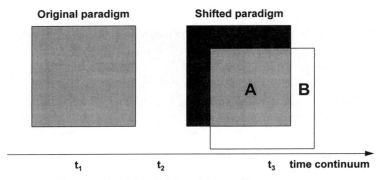

t₁: Nature of paradigm with high level of diversity in workforce
t₂: Workforce becomes more diverse at a high rate
t₃: Nature of paradigm after diversity level in workforce increases at a high rate
A = Remnant of original paradigm
B = Shifted portion of paradigm that has incorporated some of the diverse moral values
in a highly diverse workforce

Figure 4.5. Major Shift in Organization's Ethics Paradigm

have all but replaced the organization's original ethics paradigm. Point B, at Time t₃, represents the shifted portion of the organization's original ethics paradigm that has incorporated most of the diverse ethical and moral values in its highly diverse workforce.

Validity of the Model

Because very little empirical work has been done on the interface of diversity and ethics, the conceptual models presented above are primarily speculative. Also, owing to the fact that more than anecdotal yet less than empirical evidence exists to support the main premise on which these models are based (e.g., that increasing diversity in the workforce will affect organizations' ethics paradigms), arguments will undoubtedly be raised that perhaps the model infers a much greater magnitude of a problem than might actually occur. In other words, increasing diversity in the workplace may have no (or a much smaller) impact on organizations' ethics paradigms than is proposed in the models—despite the rate at which their respective workforce becomes more diverse. Moreover, arguments might be raised that the models do not consider timing. That is, assuming that a paradigm shift will occur, will it happen immediately, or over some time period?

Despite the elicitation of questions like this, the validity or usefulness of such models cannot be entirely rejected. Although the model may raise other questions, the usefulness of such models is that they provide a base from which one can begin to think critically about ethics-diversity issues. More important, the models and related discussions provided in this chapter form the foundation upon which we can begin to explore some of the practical issues related to ethics and diversity. Specifically, the models will serve as a convenient framework within which ethics-diversity issues that affect performance in the workplace can be examined. Chapter 5 is dedicated to discussions of ethics-diversity performance issues.

5

Ethics, Diversity, and Organizational Performance

There appears to be a growing conviction among U.S. businesses that a strong corporate culture, a strong commitment to ethics, and effective diversity management are vital strategic keys to organizational performance in a highly competitive environment.

The growing conviction that a strong corporate culture, ethics, and diversity management are vital strategic keys to organizational performance in a highly competitive environment is most prevalent among members of the Business Roundtable.[1] The conclusion of top executives who run organizations comprising the Business Roundtable is that, in the long run, ethical behavior results in greater organizational performance. In one of their publications, which reports on the ethical policy and practices of several large corporations, these top executives' conclusion about the relationship between ethics and organizational performance is captured in the following statement:

> It may come as a surprise to some that, as details in this report indicate, corporate ethics programs are not mounted primarily to improve the repu-

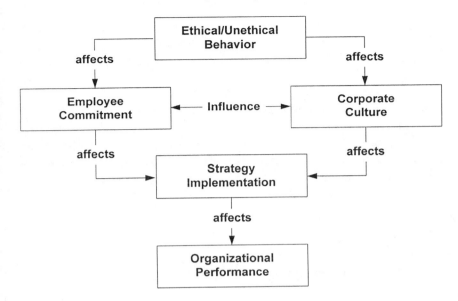

Figure 5.1. Relationship Between Ethics and Organizational Performance

tation of business. Instead, many executives believe that a culture in which ethical concern permeates the whole organization is necessary to the self-interest of the company. This is required, they feel, if the company is to be able to maintain profitability and develop the necessary competitiveness for effective performance. In the view of the top executives represented in this study, there is no conflict between ethical practice and acceptable profits. Indeed, the first is a necessary precondition for the second. Sound values, purposes, and practices are the basis for long-range achievement. (Business Roundtable, 1988, p. 9)

Although this statement does not outline the specific relationship between ethics and organizational performance (i.e., explicitly how ethical behavior leads to better performance), it does imply that corporate culture moderates the relationship in some way. As indicated in Figure 5.1, corporate culture is not the only moderator of this relationship. This model suggests that organizational ethics indirectly affects organizational performance through employee commitment and strategy implementation as well as through corporate culture.

As shown in this figure, both ethical and unethical behaviors in organizations affect corporate culture and employee commitment to the organization.

Besides having a mutual influence on one another, employee commitment and corporate culture both affect the organization's ability to successfully implement its strategy. In turn, the successful or unsuccessful implementation of strategy affects organizational performance.

In this chapter, we first explore the model presented in Figure 5.1 and then look at how shifts in organizations' ethics paradigms, caused by increasing diversity in the workplace, may lead to weaker or stronger organizational performance. The chapter concludes by looking at the work ethic of diverse groups and individuals, how it may also lead to paradigmatic shifts in ethics paradigms, and the implications for organizational performance.

◪ ETHICS AND ORGANIZATIONAL PERFORMANCE

In terms of a general definition, organizational performance is the outcome that occurs as a result of organizational behavior (Ivancevich, Szilagyi, & Wallace, 1977). Two dimensions of organizational performance have been suggested in the strategy-related literature. The first relates to the achievement of an organization's economic goals, such as growth, market share, and profitability, and the second relates to the achievement of an organization's "health-related" goals, such as worker attitudes, turnover, and morale (Fry & Killing, 1986). For the most part, both of these dimensions are achieved through an organization's strategy. The concept of strategy can be generally defined as the guiding idea of an organization or an expression of how the organization has operated, or intends to operate, in a competitive environment (Fry & Killing, 1986). As indicated in Figure 5.1, there is a direct link between the implementation of an organization's strategy and its performance. Essentially, strategy implementation is the process of translating strategy into the types of actions that result in organizational performance (Higgins & Vincze, 1993). Employees are an important part of the strategy implementation process. The model shown in Figure 5.1 indicates that employee commitment, as well as the corporate culture that is influenced by employees, affects the implementation of strategy.

The Role of Corporate Culture
and Strategy Implementation

For many activities related to the implementation of strategy, the organization may not have explicit rules indicating how employees should carry out these activities. Hence, they invariably turn to corporate culture as a source of guidance for what they should do and where to place priorities in carrying out these activities (Barney, 1986; Pearce & Robinson, 1994; Schwartz & Davis, 1981). Evidence suggests that strong corporate cultures provide clearer guidance and thus have greater impacts on the type of employee behaviors that are more directly related to successful strategy implementation (Schein, 1983).

The Role of Employee
Commitment and Implementation

It has been theorized that employees make two distinct, ongoing decisions about their commitment to an organization. The first is whether or not to participate in organizational activities, and the second is whether or not to perform at the level necessary to successfully carry out these activities (March & Simon, 1958). Decisions that relate to employee commitment to perform, at necessary levels, are most relevant to the implementation of an organization's strategy. From existing research related to organizational commitment (cf. Buchanan, 1974, 1975; O'Reilly, 1989), four major components of employee commitment to perform have been identified:

- *Internalization,* in which employees find the values of the organization to be congruent with their personal values
- *Identification* with the organization's objectives, such that employee and organizational goals are closely aligned
- *Involvement and psychological immersion* in one's work, resulting in considerable enjoyment
- *Loyalty,* perhaps even affection, toward the organization as a place to not only work but spend one's time

As suggested by this commitment-related research, these components tend to be associated with those employees who basically trust their organization and who have a clear understanding of what they are expected to do. It has been found that employees with high levels of commitment not only provide the organization with a stable and secure workforce and thus a strong corporate culture but also make the implementation of the organization's strategy more effective (Steers, 1977; Steiner & Miner, 1977).

The Role of Ethical/Unethical Behavior

Finally, the model shown in Figure 5.1 suggests that the level of employee commitment and the strength of corporate culture are both dependent on whether the behavior of the organization's employees is ethical or unethical. As an illustration of how the unethical behavior of one employee affects the commitment of other employees in an organization, consider the following incident reported by Davis and Newstrom (1985):

> A guest at a resort hotel left her camera at the information counter while she went shopping for the afternoon. The clerk placed the camera under the counter for safekeeping. When the guest returned, her camera was missing. The clerk called the manager, who investigated the situation and eventually gave the guest a $275 credit for the value of the camera. The manager determined that twenty-seven employees had access to the camera's storage place during the time that it was supposed to be there. He then applied a $10 payroll deduction to each of them for the camera, although he stated that he would return the charge if the thief confessed and paid the $275. The affected employees were angry and upset. They felt that they were being treated unfairly because they had not taken the camera but were being required to pay for someone else's unethical behavior. Most of them resented the fact that their morality had been questioned. Three employees resigned because of the incident, and two others said they would leave as soon as they could find other jobs. Employee dissatisfaction with their jobs increased and organizational performance declined. One of the employees stated that "if they are going to give us shabby treatment, then that's what we will give their guests." (pp. 47-48)

As an illustration of how unethical behavior of employees affects both employee commitment and corporate culture, Andrew Singer (1992), editor and publisher of *Ethikos,* a New York-based publication that examines ethical issues in business, related an incident experienced by a Canadian organization. According to Singer, this organization hired a consulting firm to help it with a strategy-related decision. When it was revealed that one of the organization's managers had a conflict of interest associated with implementing the strategy and that payoffs may have been involved, the CEO of the organization launched an investigation. Although the investigation concluded that there was not enough evidence to make a conviction, thus allowing the manager to keep his job, the allegation of unethical behavior "poisoned" the ethical atmosphere in the organization. The incident had such an impact on other employees that within six months of the exonerating report there was an exodus of employees from the organization.

In the first incident, unethical behavior on the part of a single employee initiated events that resulted in several employees renouncing their commitment to the organization. Based on the statement of one employee ("If they are going to give us shabby treatment, then that's what we will give their guests"), we might infer that corporate culture at the hotel was weakened by the incident. Consequently, the hotel's implied strategy of customer satisfaction was not implemented successfully and the result was decreased organizational performance. In the second incident, the mere allegation of unethical behavior essentially had the same result. What both of these incidents suggest is that unethical behavior in organizations can weaken corporate culture as well as lessen employee commitment. The opposite would also hold true. That is, ethical behavior in organizations can strengthen corporate culture as well as increase employee commitment (Deal & Kennedy, 1982; Randall, 1987).

Kenneth Andrews (1989), a noted Harvard professor, lends support to the relationship between the elements in Figure 5.1 by suggesting that the successful implementation of strategy depends on a supportive corporate culture and on the commitment of employees. He contends that employee commitment and support cannot be sustained in an environment beset by unethical behavior. The implication is that strategy implementation cannot be successful if the organization is unable to sustain employee commitment and a supportive corporate culture. Organizational performance is ultimately affected, albeit indirectly, by the impact of ethical/unethical behavior on these moderating factors.

Ethics Paradigm Shifts and Performance

A recent study (Wright, Ferris, Hiller, & Kroll, 1995) of the relationship between diversity and organizational performance found a positive link between increases in the level of diversity in the workplace and the financial performance of organizations. From an ethical perspective, this study showed that nondiscriminatory corporations tended to have more diversity in their

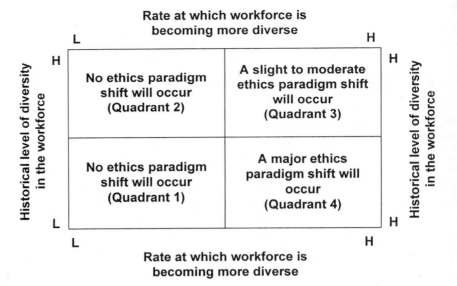

Figure 5.2. Propositions That Diversity Will Lead to Ethics Paradigm Shift

workforce. As a result, their reputation with diverse customers was enhanced, they enjoyed strong community and institutional support because of their perceived commitment to diversity, and they experienced significant increases in their financial performance.

We might infer from this study that by practicing discriminatory (unethical) or nondiscriminatory (ethical) behavior diversity will decrease or increase in organizations. Perceptions on the part of diverse employees that such behavior is indicative of the organization's attitude toward diversity may weaken or strengthen corporate culture (i.e., cause a shift in the ethics paradigm). Ultimately, organizational performance is affected either positively or negatively.

The model shown in Figure 5.2, which is a reproduction of Figure 4.2, proposes how an organization's ethics paradigm is likely to shift as a result of increasing diversity in its workforce. Quadrants 3 and 4 of this model, where, respectively, a slight-moderate or a major shift in the paradigm is likely to occur, are most relevant to performance issues in a diverse workforce. The proposed relationship between ethics paradigm shifts of this nature (i.e., slight-moderate and major) and organizational performance is shown in Figure 5.3.

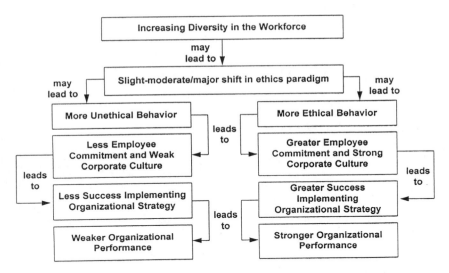

Figure 5.3. Positive and Negative Relationships Between Diversity, Ethics, and Organizational Performance

The model shown in Figure 5.3 suggests how such shifts might affect organizational performance. The model indicates that shifts in an organization's ethics paradigm, caused by increasing diversity, are not necessarily undesirable. As suggested, slight-moderate or major shifts may lead to more ethical behavior. As shown in the model, more ethical behavior may lead to greater employee commitment and a stronger corporate culture. This leads to greater success implementing organizational strategy, which, in turn, leads to stronger organizational performance. The model also suggests that when paradigmatic shifts resulting from increasing diversity lead to more unethical behavior the ultimate result is weaker organizational performance.

This model represents one way of looking at the relationship between ethics paradigm shifts, attributable to increasing diversity, and organizational performance. Another way of looking at this relationship is from the perspective of work attitudes in a diverse workforce. Such attitudes are usually assessed in terms of the work ethic, or a belief in the inherent value of work. Employees from different cultural/ethnic backgrounds may have different concepts of work, which may affect the performance of organizations with high levels of diversity in their workforce. A proposal set forth in this book is that the different (and perhaps conflicting) work ethics brought to the workplace by diversity increases may also lead to shifts in organizations' ethics paradigms. These shifts, in turn, may affect organizational performance. In the following section, we explore the relationship between diverse work ethics and organizational performance.

Diverse Work Ethics and Performance

From a religious perspective, the notion of a "work ethic" in America originated during the Protestant Reformation. The religious view of the work ethic is that work is an act of service to God and to other people because it builds a better society to help fulfill God's plan (Davis & Newstrom, 1985). Not surprising, those who subscribe to the religious perspective of the work ethic view work as a moral obligation to God. From an organizational perspective, though, studies have found that employees who possess a strong work ethic usually feel a moral commitment to achieving the types of goals that lead to organizational performance (Dubin, Champoux, & Porter, 1975; Kidron, 1978). However, not all individuals entering the workforce possess a strong work ethic. It has been argued that today, in the 1990s, most Americans view work as just another part of their life rather than as a moral benchmark (Reynolds, 1992).

At the extreme, particularly for entry-level service sector jobs, new entrants to the workforce have been described by hiring managers as lazy, unreliable, disinterested, slow, immature, and lacking a work ethic (Shimko, 1992). In a related article, James Sheedy (1990) recounted his experience observing the work ethic of teenagers and college students in a fast food restaurant. More than half of these employees were women, and one third were minorities. Sheedy commented that "for me, it was an opportunity to observe the work ethic of the future workforce—an ethic that amounted to a fierce aversion to hard work and a lack of respect for managers, customers, and often, coworkers" (p. 234).

This observed decline in the work ethic, even though the trend has been in effect for several years, comes at a time when organizations expect employees to manage themselves better and to be more productive. In other words, more value is being placed on individual performance as a means of improving organizational performance. It is the opinion of some, however, that these expectations may be out of line with reality as the workforce becomes more diverse. For example, Shimko (1992) is of the opinion that, although commonalities may exist among individuals from racially, ethnically, culturally, and otherwise diverse backgrounds, vast differences exist in factors that relate to an individual's personal work ethic (e.g., reliability, motivation, ability to influence others, and interpersonal skills).

Some of these differences are highlighted in the dimensions of culture identified by Hofstede (1980). With respect to his power distance dimension, he found that employees from low power distance countries have a stronger perceived work ethic and a strong belief that people like to work, whereas those from high power distance countries have a weaker perceived work ethic and more frequent beliefs that people dislike working. As one measure of the work ethic, Hofstede found that employees from weak uncertainty-avoidance countries and those from high-masculinity countries have a stronger achievement motivation. Employees from strong uncertainty-avoidance countries and those from low-masculinity countries have a weaker achievement motivation. These differences hold implications for organizations that may be depending on maintaining or improving performance by assuming that employees in a diverse workforce will have an equally strong work ethic.

A Managerial Perspective

For the most part, this chapter has looked at the relationship between ethics and organizational performance from an employee (nonmanagerial) perspective. The position taken was that because ethics make a difference in terms of how employees feel about themselves, their job, and the organization that employs them, ethical behavior ultimately determines their willingness to commit to the organization. Also discussed in this chapter was the idea of increasing diversity leading to more ethical behavior or more unethical behavior. From a managerial perspective, the task becomes one of how individuals in managerial roles can create an ethical climate in the midst of a workforce where ethical behavior may be dependent on how well the manager is able to deal with diversity. An argument set forth in this book is that successful completion of this task must begin with the individual manager. More specifically, those with managerial responsibility must find the principles to resolve conflicting ethical claims in their own minds and hearts before they can reconcile the ethical conflicts that may result from increasing diversity.

◥ NOTE

1. The Business Roundtable consists of 200 organizations that influence economic policy in the United States. Total employment of organizations belonging to the Business Roundtable exceeds 10 million people, and their combined sales account for nearly half of the gross national product of the United States. As a policy-setting body for business, members of this group are involved with issues related to global trade imbalances, competitiveness, and the twin deficits of trade and budget. Representative organizations include Boeing, Champion International, Chemical Bank, General Mills, GTE, Hewlett-Packard, Johnson & Johnson, McDonnell Douglas, Norton, and Xerox.

6

Managerial Ethics
and Diversity

*Effective management might be viewed as a mutually accepting
relationship between managers and their subordinates. Building this
relationship requires managerial appreciation for the personal values
and diverse traits of those willing to give their energy and talents to
accomplish shared goals.*

The way managers treat their subordinates is viewed by some as an ethical
issue (cf. Singer, 1993). Such a view can be supported by two ethics-related
principles: moral rights and distributive justice. The ethical principle of *moral
rights* would argue that employees have rights that must not be violated, and
the ethical principle of *distributive justice* centers on the concepts of fairness
and equity in the workplace (Rawls, 1971). Thus when employee rights or
justice are denied by managers, ethical violations are likely to have occurred.
With respect to diversity in the workplace, hiring and promotion practices are
often argued from the rights and justice perspectives. In a survey of 404
managers, a Harris Poll found that more than half felt that their companies
need to do a better job of hiring and promoting minorities and 44% were not

satisfied with their progress in hiring and promoting women ("Harris Executive Poll," 1991).

In a more recent study, the American Management Association (AMA, 1995) surveyed 983 managers and sought their opinion about the promotion practices of their respective company, with respect to diversity. One question on the survey was "Are minorities overlooked for key promotions?" In a comparative 1992 survey conducted by the AMA, 21% of the managers responded "always" or "often" to this question, whereas in the 1995 survey, only 11% of the managers did so. In support of this trend toward a positive opinion toward promoting minorities, this same study found that the percentage of minorities in the frontline management cadre increased from 14.5% in 1992 to 19.3% in 1995. The percentage in middle management increased from 11.2% in 1992 to 15.1% in 1995, and the percentage in senior management increased from 7.4% in 1992 to 10.6% in 1995.

Generally, results of the AMA studies suggest that U.S. companies are doing a better job in the area of hiring and promoting individuals from diverse racial, cultural, and ethnic backgrounds. However, the relatively low percentage changes in the AMA studies along with the percentage of managers indicating that their companies only did a fair or poor job hiring, promoting, and retaining women and minorities (cf. "Harris Executive Poll," 1991), suggest that the principles of rights and justice may be an emerging ethical issue among managers in organizations where diversity is a growing concern.

Many of the cases in Part 2 of this book deal with some practical implications of the rights and justice principles. In this chapter, however, the focus is on the personal ethics of managers as they attempt to manage a diverse workforce. Particular emphasis is placed on the dilemma faced by white male managers, who may feel displaced by diversity but are expected to maintain moral integrity in their interactions with employees from different racial, ethnic, cultural, and otherwise diverse backgrounds.

◪ THE ETHNIC MINORITY PERSPECTIVE

At Levi Strauss & Company, a set of corporate "aspirations" was written by top management to guide decisions related to diversity and ethics (Mitchell

& O'Neal, 1994). This company's diversity aspiration states that Levi Strauss "values a diverse workforce (age, sex, ethnic group, etc.) at all levels of the organization. . . . Differing points of view will be sought; diversity will be valued and honestly rewarded, not suppressed" (p. 47). An associated ethical aspiration states that Levi Strauss management should epitomize "the stated standards of ethical behavior. We must provide clarity about our expectations and must enforce these standards throughout the corporation" (p. 47). According to these aspirations, management at Levi Strauss will not conduct business with those (e.g., suppliers and intermediate customers) who violate the company's strict standards regarding their position on diversity and ethics. Although several other companies have taken a similar position, not all U.S. companies have come around to this enlightened view.

Ethics in Hiring Ethnic Minorities

Many companies hire just enough ethnic minorities to satisfy the government, and many have learned to give ethnic minorities, homosexuals, women, foreign-born individuals, and others hiring preferences to protect themselves against discrimination suits. Once hired, though, these groups contend that they often receive unfair treatment from their managers. At Monsanto Company, for instance, the problem was not in hiring individuals from these diverse groups but retaining them (Ellis, 1991). In 1988, women and minorities were quietly leaving Monsanto at a disproportionate rate. In a series of detailed exit interviews, 100% of the ethnic minorities who left reported experiencing difficulty with their managers. They felt that treatment by their managers seemed arbitrary and unfair. The exit interviews revealed equally damning comments from departing female employees. Twenty percent more women than men said they were treated unfairly concerning pay and promotion decisions.

Ethics in Promoting Ethnic Minorities

With respect to diversity and promotion practices, particularly promotions into managerial positions, nearly 97% of higher-level managers in the largest U.S. organizations are white males. Blacks make up 12.7% of the private sector workforce, but only 5% of all U.S. managers are black (Gleckman, Smart, Dwyer, Segal, & Weber, 1991). Similarly, Hispanics make up 7.5% of the workforce but hold only 4% of white-collar jobs. Instead, they tend to perform agricultural, janitorial, and other types of menial labor (Dwyer & Cuneo, 1991). In contrast, Asian Americans face less resistance in getting hired for white-collar jobs. One of their unique problems is the widely held stereotype that they are hard workers but are not assertive enough to be managers.

The seeming distaste for hiring and promoting minorities might be traced to stereotyping as well as the deep vein of prejudice that runs through the management cadre of some organizations. As an illustration, the manager of one company hired a black women, basing his decision on a personal desire "to do the right thing." Yet when he passed her over for a promotion, she sued, claiming race discrimination. Consequently, the manager says that he will not hire other blacks (Gleckman et al., 1991). Another company's manager stated that he has had blacks on his payroll for years and has been fully satisfied with their work. Yet he refuses to actively recruit them, his reason being that "it's not like it was in the old days when you gave a black man a job and he appreciated it and didn't try to stir things up" (Gleckman et al., 1991, p. 60).

From the perspective of diverse individuals in organizations, the consensus appears to be that when it comes to hiring and promotions the tendency is for white male managers to pick white males for key positions. Managers that engage in this type of unethical behavior no doubt risk inflaming dissension and hurting morale and productivity. On the other hand, the shifting dynamics of the workforce have placed many white male managers in a moral quandary. In their efforts to make their organizations more diverse, they are certain to hire or promote women and minorities over other white males.

▨ THE WHITE MALE PERSPECTIVE

In the past, Corporate America was populated mainly by what has been called "corporate cultural natives" (Butler, 1993). In other words, white, Anglo-Saxon, Protestant, heterosexual men of at least average height with corresponding weight and no visible physical impairments. This historic white male stereotype once defined the appearance, traits, values, and behaviors of the ideal manager. It has been suggested that this stereotype has resulted in overt or subtle discrimination in selection, evaluation, and promotion practices (Mandell & Kohler-Gray, 1990). That is, because women and minorities striving for management positions cannot live up to this ideal they are frequently passed over. However, many organizations are beginning to discard the old stereotype of the ideal manager and beginning to embrace the idea that good managers come in both genders, in all ages, and in all racial, ethnic, and cultural types (Mandell & Kohler-Gray, 1990). As suggested by Butler (1993), the "corporate cultural natives" (i.e., white males) are being replaced by "corporate cultural foreigners" (i.e., women, minorities, and immigrants).

As evidence of this cultural shift, between 1983 and 1993 the percentage of white male professionals and managers in the workforce dropped from 55% to 47%, whereas the percentage of white women in similar positions increased from 37% to 42% (Galen & Palmer, 1994). The consequence, though, has been feelings of frustration and resentment among white male managers, which have been manifested in their filing internal complaints about unfair treatment. The ethical concepts of rights and justice are relevant to this situation. On the one hand, white male managers are expected to exercise their moral obligation toward diversity by respecting all employees' rights and administering rules fairly and enforcing them impartially. Many times, however, they find that providing promotional opportunities for a member of a minority group or for a woman means that a white male employee with perhaps more seniority or who may be more qualified is deprived of an advancement opportunity. On the other hand, the wave of employee rights and justice issues surrounding diversity will likely compel organizations to respond in a socially responsible manner. During the process, the white male may find that his own rights are overshadowed or that justice is not forthcoming.

For organizations committed to a corporate culture that embraces diversity, this situation raises the dilemma of how to ensure a diverse workforce without violating the rights of white males while ensuring that white male managers behave ethically toward their diverse charges. According to Solomon (1991), the ethical question becomes "How do you ameliorate past inequities toward women, minorities, the aged, homosexuals, and others without penalizing and embittering another very important component of the workforce?" This question is particularly relevant to lower-level managers who spend a significant amount of time directing and monitoring the activities of others. These managers make decisions about work assignments, promotions, discipline, and performance evaluations. In a diverse workforce, they are likely to be confronted by racially, ethnically, culturally, and otherwise diverse individuals who are concerned with ethical issues related to fairness, equity, and their rights as employees.

▧ CROSS-CULTURAL PERSPECTIVES

Some management and labor experts have warned that the ethics-related issues of rights and justice could become a major social and economic issue as more foreign-owned companies begin to conduct business in the United States (Permutter & Heenan, 1984). Some well-known foreign-owned companies with operations in the United States are Dillard Department Stores and Shell Oil (The Netherlands), Volkswagen of America and Spiegel, Inc. (Germany), First Boston Bank (Switzerland), Firestone Tire and Rubber, California First Bank, and National Steel (Japan), American Motors, Total Petroleum, and Mack Trucks (France), and Barclay's Bank, United Bank of Arizona, and Keebler (United Kingdom). With respect to staffing their operations, many of these companies have adopted geocentric attitudes. This means that managers from these companies' country of origin are assigned to oversee and manage their U.S.-based operations.

For many foreign companies that have operations in the United States and for the managers they assign here, there are important cultural differences in attitudes about hiring women and how they are treated once they are in the workplace. This is particularly true of Arab and Asian managers due to the fact that women face many social restrictions in their home country. The same type of treatment may be extended to U.S. minorities in the workplace of these countries, whose managers likely have very little or no experience in hiring and managing the different ethnic minorities found in the U.S. workforce.

The experience of Japanese managers in the United States might be used as a representative example of how cultural differences can result in the emergence of rights and justice issues in a diverse workforce. For instance, in 1986 international attention was focused on the plight of minorities in Japanese companies based in the United States when Yasuhire Kakasone, who was then Japan's prime minister, suggested that blacks, Hispanics, and other minorities pull down educational levels in the United States (Frantz, 1988). Partly due to Mr. Nakasone's remarks, Japanese hiring and promotion practices in the

United States attracted the scrutiny of the Equal Employment Opportunity Commission (EEOC), the federal agency that monitors compliance with antidiscrimination laws. In 1988, the Commission announced that a pattern of discrimination had been found at the U.S. manufacturing division of Honda, located in Marysville, Ohio. The company agreed to pay $6 million to black employees as a result of past discrimination in hiring and promotion.

Japanese managers' record of hiring and promoting women was found to be no better than their record of hiring and promoting minorities. This finding is likely related to the role of women in the Japanese workforce. Only recently has a women's movement begun in Japan, and women managers are rare. A survey of 310,000 junior managers in Japan found that less than .05% were women (Frantz, 1988). A study conducted by New York's Columbia University Graduate School of Business found that only 2% of the management positions in Japanese-owned companies in the United States were held by women in 1985, a figure that was unchanged from 1982 (Frantz, 1988). In a related study, the Council on Economic Priorities, a nonprofit research organization in New York, found no women among 1,493 managers working for five diversified Japanese companies located in the United States. (Frantz, 1988).

In a recent development (Schilling & Neuborne, 1996), the EEOC charged the U.S. subsidiary of Mitsubishi Motor Manufacturing of America, a Japanese-owned company, with creating "a hostile and abusive work environment" at its plant in Normal, Illinois. The EEOC charge alleged that women were groped, grabbed, and touched and forced out of their jobs if they complained. Japanese managers at Mitsubishi announced in June 1996 that an independent investigation, led by former Secretary of Labor Lynn Martin, would produce specific steps to improve the work environment for women and minorities at its U.S. operations as early as mid-July 1996.

The fact that more foreign-born managers are practicing in the United States is not entirely due to the number of foreign-owned companies conducting business here. To instill a more global orientation, American Standard Inc., a large New York-based manufacturer, began to recruit foreign managers to run its key U.S. operations. As a result, nearly one third of all vice presidential positions at the company's corporate headquarters have been filled by foreign-born personnel ("American Standard's Executive Melting Pot," 1993).

With respect to employee rights and justice, the concept of equal opportunity is much more advanced in the United States than in most other countries. As managers from countries where this concept is not fully developed assume managerial positions in U.S. companies, there may be more instances where violations of the ethical principles of rights and justice occur.

◪ THE LEGAL PERSPECTIVE

Whether American-born or from some other country, managers of U.S. organizations are not completely free to choose who they hire or promote. Legally, they have an ethical responsibility not to violate the principles of rights and justice. That is, decisions to hire and promote must be made without regard to race, gender, religion, age, color, or national origin. Three major pieces of legislation—Age Discrimination in Employment Act, Americans with Disabilities Act, and the Civil Rights Act—were designed to prevent violations of rights and justice principles. These three laws cover just about every aspect of diversity. For example, the Civil Rights Act prohibits discrimination based on race, color, religion, gender, or national origin. The Age Discrimination in Employment Act prohibits age discrimination against employees between 40 and 65 years of age. And the Americans with Disabilities Act prohibits discrimination against individuals with physical or mental disabilities or the chronically ill.

Despite the existence of these laws, they have only helped reduce but not completely eliminate violations of the rights and justice principles. Similar to arguments presented in an earlier chapter, that ethical conduct can only be determined by each individual's personal code of conduct and not by an organization's code of ethics, the argument set forth in this chapter is that a manager's value orientation ultimately determines whether he or she will violate these two principles. This ethical/moral approach to managing in a diverse workplace is more in keeping with the deontological perspective on ethics, which implies that the manager does the right thing simply because it is right and not because of any regulatory consequences.

◪ THE ROLE OF MANAGERIAL VALUES

The ethics-related theories of rights and justice tell us only that employees have rights that must not be violated and that they should be treated fairly and equitably. However, these theories do not tell us how rights and justice should be balanced in practical management situations. In the absence of normative theories prescribing how managers might achieve this balance, their personal values must suffice. Some managers hold deep convictions about the intrinsic worth of all employees and the importance of relating to them in ways that express that conviction. This personal conviction (or value) will influence not only how the manager deals directly with a diverse workforce but the kind of decisions likely to be made when faced with competing choices. For example, a decision by a white male manager to promote a minority or a woman over another white male whom he has been grooming for that particular promotion might be influenced by his personal value system.

As opposed to personal values, it has been argued that other managers may be motivated primarily by economic values (Williams, DuBrin, & Sisk, 1985). Although these managers' deepest concerns are creating a productive workforce and promoting their own success, they also have strong beliefs about how employees should be treated. As an outgrowth of their economic values they may seek a balance between ensuring customer satisfaction, which may require a demanding approach toward managing, and ensuring that employees are treated with dignity at all times. A personal value system that leads a manager to hold deep convictions about the intrinsic worth of all employees clearly reflects an "enlightened" approach to managing, whereas a manager who is directed by economic values clearly subscribes to an "enlightened self-interest" approach to managing. Within the context of diversity, both of these value systems are capable of producing managerial behavior that is highly ethical or moral as judged by the most demanding external standards.

Another way of looking at managerial values has been suggested by England (1975). He compared American managers with managers from Japan, Korea, Australia, and India on two different value orientations that are related to ethics and diversity. The first orientation, the *pragmatic approach,* is consistent with a teleological perspective on ethics. Managers with this value orientation tend to evaluate their behavior toward diversity in terms of the consequences the behavior produces. Subsequently, if they feel that there will be regulatory consequences (e.g., affirmative action sanctions) forthcoming if the principles of rights and justice are violated, they will likely behave more ethically toward a diverse workforce. With respect to the proportion of managers, of those who hold the pragmatic value orientation, American managers (57.3%) are second behind Japanese managers (67.4%) and ahead of Korean (53.1%), Australian (40.2%), and Indian managers (34%).

The second value orientation, the *ethical/moral approach,* is consistent with the deontological perspective on ethics. Managers with this value orientation engage in ethical behavior because they feel that it is the right thing to do. Thus these managers would not intentionally or knowingly violate the rights and justice principles. Moral obligation, not fear of regulatory consequences, motivates them to behave ethically toward a diverse workforce. A higher percentage of Indian (44.1%), Australian (40,2%), and American managers (30.3%) hold this value orientation, whereas a significantly lower percentage of Korean (9%) and Japanese managers (9.9%) subscribe to it. Both of these value orientations hold implications for how managers are likely to treat individuals that make up a diverse workforce.

At least one business ethicist is of the view that

> individuals who are similar in all respects relevant to the kind of treatment in question should be given similar benefits and burdens, even if they are dissimilar in other irrelevant respects; and individuals who are dissimilar in a relevant respect ought to be treated dissimilarly, in proportion to their dissimilarity. (Velasquez, 1982, p. 46)

The message conveyed in this quote is that the moral right of employees to be treated as free and equal persons undergirds the notion that managers should adopt a bias-free approach to managing employees in a diverse workforce. As suggested by some, there is little doubt that such a bias-free approach along with the ethical relationships that managers establish in dealing with others arise from their value system (Anderson, 1984). Differences in managers' value systems will contribute greatly to differences in how they manage within the context of diversity. These differences will become greater as managers from diverse racial, ethnic, cultural, and otherwise diverse backgrounds assume managerial positions in U.S. organizations. Eventually though, through the corporate value system and its ethical codes these differences should begin to coalesce such that uniform behavior toward rights and justice are established.

▨ ETHICS, DIVERSITY, AND MANAGERIAL EFFECTIVENESS

When all managers begin to understand that ethical treatment of employees is a critical dimension of their own effectiveness and/or organizational success, managing ethically in a diverse workforce will become an entrenched managerial value. The task, however, is facilitating such an understanding. In the next chapter, the focus is on methods that organizations might use to reconcile ethical differences in a diverse workforce. The methods discussed are designed to promote the type of understanding that will lead to more ethical behavior on the part of managers as they interact with employees from diverse origins.

Reconciling Diverse Ethical Values

Once organizations have developed an understanding of the terrain of existing ethics and values and the points of difference, all that is left for them to do is work out how the diverse ethics and values can be reconciled without compromising their own core values and ethics.

Culturally, racially, and ethnically diverse individuals are likely carriers of ethical values that are different from those subscribed to by mainstream America. There are a limited number of ways in which these carriers can affect the ethics of mainstream America and a limited number of ways to respond. One suggested response is "infiltration" (Buller, Kohls, & Anderson, 1991). This response suggests that by slowly or systematically introducing culturally, racially, ethnically, or otherwise diverse individuals into the ethic of mainstream America the idea may spread to others. Another response, "accommodation," suggests that these carriers might merely adapt to the ethic of mainstream America, and, similarly, mainstream America may adopt the ethic of these carriers (Buller et al., 1991).

Although these responses may apply to carriers and mainstream America, more proactive responses may be necessary for organizations. It has been argued that productive organizations need to find ways to inculcate ethics in the workplace, and this necessitates a systematic outlook (Madsen, 1991). What this means in terms of diversity is that organizations must formulate proactive strategies for creating ethical synergy. Such strategies would build upon similarities and fuse differences, using diverse individuals to help reconcile ethics-related conflicts through combined action. In this chapter, strategies designed to create ethical synergy in organizations are presented. This chapter begins by considering the role of human resources management in creating ethical synergy and concludes by considering the role of leadership.

◩ THE ROLE OF HUMAN RESOURCES MANAGEMENT

Human resources management (HRM) has been generally defined as the the process of placing the right people with the right skills in the right place at the right time, with the right motivation, to achieve organizational objectives (Schuler, Galiente, & Jackson, 1987). One of the initial steps in this process is recruiting and selecting potential employees to satisfy the organization's human resource needs. It has been noted that some organizations are extremely rigorous in their selection process . In a study of several organizations, for instance, Pascale (1985) found that candidates for employment were subjected to a selection process so rigorous that it often seemed designed to discourage rather than encourage the candidates to take the job. The reason for such rigor in the process is to increase the chances of selecting potential employees whose values are highly congruent with those embodying the organization's corporate culture (Jones, 1986).

Of special concern to HRM is ensuring that those individuals selected for employment are molded into the type of employees who can abide by the organization's corporate culture (Pascale, 1985). The ultimate purpose of this molding process is to change the values of those selected to match the value system subscribed to by the organization's corporate culture (Higgins, 1991). As suggested in Figure 7.1, individuals having high congruency with the organization's value system are selected first because they are most likely to abide by the organization's corporate culture. Those individuals whose values are only marginally congruent with the organization's value system are also

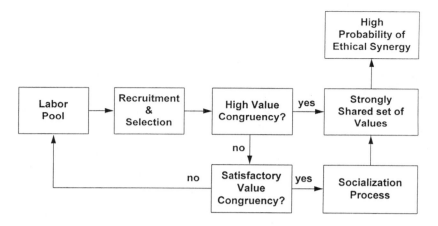

Figure 7.1. The Role of HRM in Reconciling Individual-Organizational Values

selected but are put through a molding process. If the HRM task is successfully completed, employees will strongly share in a commonly held set of values. In turn, the probability is high that the organization will achieve ethical synergy.

HRM and Ethical Synergy

Unfortunately, the task of HRM is not always successful. The need to meet human resources requirements is often given priority over selection rigor. Consequently, many of those individuals selected for employment may hold values that are not even satisfactorily congruent with the organization's value system. It must be noted, however, that HRM professionals do not operate in a vacuum and environmental changes that affect their job may occur faster than they can adjust. Moreover, the prevailing value system of organizations often is implicit, and so a challenge to HRM professionals is to recognize how many assumptions about ethical behavior are buried within corporate culture.

What this means is that as the labor pool begins to fill with racially, culturally, ethnically, and otherwise diverse individuals, more systematic approaches to carrying out the HRM task must be developed. Cross-cultural research suggests that current HRM paradigms neglect the potential impact that diversity might have on organizations (Laurent, 1983). This line of research suggests that human resource (HR) managers are of the opinion that a strong corporate culture moderates the effect of diverse values that individuals bring to the workplace.

The assumption is that employees, even if they are from different ethnic, cultural, or racial backgrounds, leave their socially instilled values at the portal as they enter the workplace. If they do not, the assumption is that the prevailing corporate culture will neutralize potential influences that their values might have on the organization's value system. Subsequently, new hires (cultural, racial, and ethnic backgrounds notwithstanding) are expected to respond to situations within the organization in ways that are consistent with the prevailing value system. It has been argued that when organizations operate on such assumptions, new entrants to their workforce are given great latitude to make differentiated responses to situations that occur within the organization (Jones, 1986). Innovative responses are a likely result, which may not be consistent with the prevailing value system. Such responses may tend to weaken the set of values shared by organizational members and thus lower the probability that ethical synergy will be achieved. The next few sections of this chapter focus on an HRM framework that will help organizations move toward achieving ethical synergy within the context of diversity.

Toward an HRM Framework

The four major cultural dimensions developed by Hofstede (1980), along which societies differ, were presented in Chapter 3. The first dimension, power distance, is the degree to which a society accepts inequalities in organizational relationships. It has been suggested that in cultures where the degree of power distance is low or moderate, individuals look more to their peers than to their superiors for guidance in terms of ethical conduct (Ferrell, Zey-Ferrell, & Krugman, 1983).

The second dimension, uncertainty avoidance, is the degree to which individuals in a society feel threatened by situations that are unstructured, unclear, or unpredictable. Individuals from cultures where the level of uncertainty avoidance is low may sometimes accept unethical behavior when there is no formal standard or rule to guide behavior (Ferrell & Skinner, 1988).

The third dimension, individualism/collectivism, refers to the extent to which individuals in a society view themselves as individuals or as part of a larger group. Studies have shown that ethical/unethical behavior in organizations is sometimes determined by the extent to which individuals consider the group as being more important than themselves (Hegarty & Sims, 1979; Robin & Reidenbach, 1987). Such individuals are usually from cultures where the individualism dimension is low.

Table 7.1   Relationship Between National and Corporate Culture

Major National Cultural Dimensions	Major Corporate Cultural Dimensions
1a. Power Distance →→→→→→→→→→→→	1b. Organizational Control
2a. Uncertainty Avoidance →→→→→→→→→	2b. Risk Behavior
3a. Individualism-Collectivism →→→→→→→	3b. Individual Autonomy
4a. Masculinity-Femininity →→→→→→→→→	4b. Reward Orientation

DEFINITIONS

1a. Degree to which a nation/region encourages unequal distribution of power among its people.

1b. Degree to which organizations in the nation/region use direct supervision to control employee behavior.

2a. Degree to which people in the nation/region feel threatened by unstable and ambiguous situations and try to avoid them.

2b. Degree to which organizations in the nation/region encourage employees to be aggressive, innovative, and risk-seeking.

3a. Degree to which individuals or groups are used to solve the nation/region's problems.

3b. Degree to which organizations in the nation/region allow employees to have responsibility, independence, and opportunities for exercising initiative.

4a. Degree to which the dominant values of the nation/region emphasize achievement, assertiveness, and high performance.

4b. Degree to which incentives offered by organizations in the nation/region are based on high employee performance.

The fourth dimension, masculinity/femininity, is the extent to which a society's dominant values emphasize assertiveness and materialism versus concern for people and quality of life. A major implication stemming from this dimension is that the focus on materialism in some masculine cultures may contribute significantly to an individual's propensity to engage in unethical behavior.

Developing the HRM Framework

In developing an HRM framework for creating ethical synergy, a connection between these four dimensions of (national) culture and corresponding

Table 7.2   Different Cultural Clusters

Cluster	Sample Countries Comprising Cluster
Anglo-American	United States, Canada, Australia, New Zealand, United Kingdom, Ireland South Africa
Latin European	France, Belgium, Italy, Portugal, Spain
Latin American	Argentina, Venezuela, Chile, Mexico, Peru, Colombia
Far Eastern	Malaysia, Hong Kong, China, Singapore, Philippines, South Vietnam, Indonesia, Taiwan, Thailand
Arab	Abu-Dhabi, Oman, Bahrain, United Arab Emirates, Kuwait, Saudi Arabia
Near Eastern	Turkey, Iran, Greece
Nordic	Finland, Norway, Denmark, Sweden
Germanic	Austria, Germany, Switzerland
Independent	Brazil, Japan, India, Israel

SOURCE: Based on Hofstede (1980).

dimensions of corporate culture must be made. Inferences drawn from research studies (cf. Campbell, Dunnette, Lawler, & Weick, 1970; Davis, 1957; Forehand & Gilmer, 1964; Likert, 1967; Payne & Pugh, 1976) are that a direct link exists between Hofstede's dimensions of national culture and the dimensions of corporate culture shown in Table 7.1. Suggested in this table is that the relative position of the national culture dimensions on a high-low continuum corresponds directly to the relative position of the corporate culture dimensions on the same high-low continuum.

Given the number of cultures there are to consider, developing a practical HRM framework would require HR managers to use the cultural clusters identified in Chapter 3. Table 7.2 is a reproduction of Table 3.5, which contains a sample of cultural clusters and a sample of countries comprising each cluster. Each cluster's relative position on each dimension of national culture must be known also. Table 7.3, which is a reproduction of Table 3.6, indicates where each cluster is positioned on each dimension. This knowledge will allow HR managers to assess their organization's relative position on corresponding corporate culture dimensions.

The objective of such an assessment is to make HR managers more effective in terms of selecting individuals whose values are congruent with the organization's value system. Using the information provided in Table 7.2 and

Table 7.3 Cultural Clusters and Dimensions

Cultural Dimension				
Cultural Cluster	Individualism[a]	Power Distance	Uncertainty Avoidance	Masculinity[b]
Anglo-American	High	Low/Moderate	Low	High
Germanic	Moderate	Low	Moderate/High	Moderate/High
Nordic	Moderate/High	Low	Low/Moderate	Low
Near Eastern	Low	High	High	Moderate
Arab	Low	High	Moderate/High	Moderate
Far Eastern	Low	High	Low/Moderate	Moderate
Latin American	Low	High	High	High
Latin European	High	High	High	High

[a]Low individualism is equivalent to Collectivism
[b]Low Masculinity is equivalent to Femininity

SOURCE: Based on Hofstede (1980).

Table 7.3, HR managers would first determine their corporate culture's relative position on the high-low dimensions shown in Table 7.3. In regard to American organizations, they would fall into the Anglo-American cultural cluster. Thus their "generalized" corporate culture would be high on the individual autonomy dimension (refer to Table 7.1), low/moderate on the organization control dimension, low on the risk behavior dimension, and high on the reward orientation dimension. From this determination, HR managers will have developed what might be called a "generalized corporate culture profile" (GCCP).

Applying the HRM Framework

The next step would be to develop a GCCP for each cultural cluster and compare it to the organization's own GCCP. To fulfill the organization's human resource needs, initial recruitment efforts would target individuals from those cultural clusters whose GCCP is congruent with the organization's own GCCP. Within the context of diversity, high levels of congruency in each recruit may not be obtainable when selecting from the labor pool. If the labor pool consists mainly of individuals from cultures where there is not a high level of congruency with the organization's GCCP yet human resource needs must be met, the strategy of "nonpassive socialization" will have to be adopted.

It has been suggested that new hires are not usually provided with information and programs designed to help them better understand what values are consistent with the prevailing corporate culture; they are passively socialized into the organization's value system (Laurent, 1983). Passive socialization (i.e., learning the organization's value system by following the example of others) may take longer than desired to coalesce values in a diverse workplace. For example, one study (Hopkins & Hopkins, 1990) found that when passive socialization is used it can take from 8 to 11 years for individuals from several different cultures to reach congruency with American-born employees on the dimensions of culture identified by Hofstede.

The nonpassive approach focuses on rapidly integrating diverse individuals into the organization's value system. This is done through formal methods such as building their language skills so that values can be easily transmitted and assigning diverse individuals formal mentors to reinforce organizational values. This process represents an effective way of rapidly reconciling diverse values to the value system embodied in the organization's corporate culture.

Kenichi Ohmae (1989) philosophized that the culture of an organization is like soil, in which similar kinds of crops are grown. If an organization tries to grow incompatible crops in this soil, they will never reap a proper long-term harvest. This philosophy captures the essence of the HRM framework discussed in this chapter. Because of increasing diversity, organizations will find themselves planting incompatible crops (diverse ethical values) in their cultural soil. As a result, they may find themselves faced with the task of trying to reap a long-term harvest of ethical synergy without the appropriate harvesting implements. The HRM framework discussed in this section might be viewed as one implement that can be used to help organizations achieve this synergy.

Regulation Versus Reconciliation

Generally implied in the HRM framework is that a desired result is to reconcile the ethical values of diverse individuals to the ethical values subscribed to by the organization. Although such a reconciliation may be desirable, it may not be expedient and may have legal implications. In terms of expediency, it was suggested earlier that it can take several years for the values of individuals from different cultures to be reconciled with the values of a host culture. Legally, laws such as Affirmative Action and Equal Employment

Opportunity may place limitations on how stringently the selection process is carried out. The possibility of discriminatory practices entering into the process may subject HR managers to greater scrutiny under these laws, particularly within the context of increasing diversity.

The point to be grasped here is that the effectiveness of the HRM framework in reconciling diverse ethical values may be reduced because of legal constraints. Yet, despite its limitations, the HRM framework is a useful tool for reconciling diverse ethical values when other strategies are used in conjunction with it. Regulating ethical behavior in a diverse workforce through codification and supervisory involvement represents one such strategy that has broad support in the literature.

Ethical Codes Revisited

The notion that what may be considered ethical in one culture may be considered unethical in another has been reinforced throughout this book. Such a notion implies that when individuals from diverse racial, ethnic, cultural, and otherwise diverse backgrounds enter the workplace, many of them may not know what organizational behaviors are considered ethical or unethical. Therefore, it is incumbent upon the organization to take the initiative to publicize clear ethical standards to its workforce. For many organizations, these standards are set forth in corporate codes of ethics. Although some individuals in a diverse workforce may come from cultures or backgrounds where one's moral sense is preferred over written codes, corporate codes of ethics can serve the purpose of guiding behavior and clarifying ethical responsibilities (Madsen, 1991). Once the code is explicitly presented to the workforce, ignorance of what is ethical or unethical behavior cannot be used by individuals as a viable defense for their actions.

What should be in the code? Business ethicists (e.g., Harrington, 1991) suggest that corporate codes of ethics should be specific policy-type documents that cover most fundamental areas of concern. A nonexhaustive enumeration of these areas include the following: conflicts of interest, illegal conduct, inappropriate gifts to corporate personnel, safeguarding company assets, honesty in business communication, sexual harassment, whistleblowing, gift giving, entertainment and travel, governmental contracting responsibilities, unauthorized payments to foreign officials, drug and alcohol abuse, affirmative action, employee privacy, environmental issues, product and workplace safety, employee health screening, security of company records, and shareholder interests. Besides these specific areas of concern, Karp and Abramms (1992) suggest that codes of ethics have at least four characteristics:

- *Be visible*—If a diverse workforce will be subjected to a code of ethics, they must be aware that it exists. Therefore, the code should be widely circulated and posted.
- *Reflect organizational values*—Because the code is the vehicle through which diverse individuals will become familiar with the organization's ethical identity, it must reflect the value system of the organization.
- *Support individual values*—Inevitably, individuals in a diverse workforce will not hold exactly the same standards for right and wrong as those held by the organization. Although the code establishes the outer limits of acceptable behavior, it cannot be functional unless it represents the ethical standards of most members of the workforce.
- *Focus on behavior*—To state ethics in anything but behavioral terms may translate into an attack on diverse individuals' personal values and beliefs. Therefore, the code should focus only on ethical behaviors that can be judged against published standards.

To reinforce corporate codes of ethics and to strengthen the personal ethical framework of a diverse workforce, it has been suggested that organizations devote more resources to ethics training programs (Sims, 1992). These programs should explain the underlying ethical and legal principles of the code and present practical aspects of carrying out procedural guidelines (Drake and Drake, 1988). This helps members of a diverse workforce clarify their own ethical frameworks as well as allow them to practice self-discipline in adhering to the written code.

Supervisory Involvement

Reinforcing ethical behavior in a diverse workforce also falls within the purview of supervisors. Their focus is on the institutionalization of ethical norms and practices that are incorporated in the corporate code. In what might be called a "diversity sensitive" approach to involving themselves in regulatory matters, business ethicists (e.g., Hodgson, 1992) have suggested several strategies that immediate supervisors might adopt. From a personal perspective, it has been suggested that they (a) become more sensitive to the customs, values, and practices of other peoples, which they themselves view as moral, traditional, practical, and effective; (b) do not judge the values of diverse individuals as necessarily immoral, corrupt, or primitive but assume they are legitimate until proved otherwise; and (c) find legitimate ways to operate from their ethical points of view but do not demand that they operate only by the supervisory point of view if insignificant differences exist between the two.

Along with these three recommendations it has been suggested that supervisors always exercise ethical conduct when working with diverse individuals (Holmquist, 1993). That is, they should (a) treat all employees equally yet make allowances for individual differences, (b) recognize each person as an individual with feelings, rights, and responsibilities, (c) understand that the more these diverse individuals succeed in gaining their own recognition the better will be their "ethics" or "standard of conduct," and (c) understand that bias or prejudice can impede the effectiveness of any supervisor. Finally, Holmquist (1993) suggests that supervisors in a diverse workforce will often have the opportunity to act in the capacity of a teacher. This may entail inculcating ethics in the workplace via one-on-one instruction. Therefore, supervisors must remember that their students may come in all sizes, shapes, colors, and abilities, which may require an adjustment in their teaching presentation and style.

The Role of Leadership

Research studies (e.g., Arlow & Ulrich, 1980; Posner & Schmidt, 1984; Touche-Ross Foundation, 1988; Vitell & Festervand, 1987) clearly support the conclusion that the ethical philosophies of leaders can have a major impact on the ethical behavior of their followers. As leaders, the ethical philosophies of an organization's top managers will have little impact on employees' ethical behavior unless the philosophies are supported by managerial behaviors that are consistent with these philosophies. In other words, top managers must model their commitment to institutionalizing ethics in both work and deed.

As noted by one ethicist, "Nothing sends a louder signal than leadership clearly stating that ethics is a priority, an issue that must be addressed by everyone in the organization" (Madsen, 1991, p. 11). Such a signal may have a particularly profound impact on individuals from cultures where the power distance between management and subordinates is large. Their strict adherence to the organization's ethical norms, as embodied in its codes and reinforced through supervisory involvement, is much more likely if support and care about ethical practices emanates from the top of the organization. In short, top managers must be aware that they are role models, for the most powerful positive influence toward ethical behavior in a diverse workforce is an ethical leader.

Implications for Business Ethics

Concern about civil and equal rights in an increasingly diverse society and workforce will no doubt lead to a drastic change in the "rules of the game" by which U.S. business is expected to operate.

The concept of business ethics has been described as a type of applied ethics that is primarily concerned with clarifying the obligations of organizational participants (e.g., managers and nonmanagerial personnel) who make business decisions (Buchholz, 1989). Business ethicists (e.g., Madsen & Shafritz, 1990) tend to divide the field of business ethics into two separate areas. The first area, called *mischief*, concerns the illegal, unethical, or questionable practices of organizational participants as well as the causes of such practices and remedies available to prevent or eradicate them. Activities such as fraud and consumer deception, kickbacks and bribery, insider trading, government contracting improprieties, conflicts of interest, questionable advertising claims, illegal disposal of hazardous materials, intentional violations of workplace safety regulations, and laundering of drug-trafficking money by financial institutions represent the types of ethical mischief that organizational participants might find themselves involved in.

The second area, called *moral mazes* (Madsen & Shafritz, 1990), concerns the moral philosophy and moral reasoning of organizational participants. This second area can be divided into two levels: *macro moral mazes* and *micro moral mazes*. Essentially, macro moral mazes are ethical issues that have sweeping implications for companies and society, and micro moral mazes are ethical issues limited to individuals within a company. Macro and micro moral mazes that confront organizational participants generally encompass issues such as conflict of interest in the workplace, employee rights, fair performance appraisals, sexual harassment, proprietary information, confidentiality, discrimination, corporate social responsibility, product liability, environmental ethics, multinational and transnational ethics, comparable worth, layoffs and downsizings, employee screening tests, privacy in the workplace, and corporate accountability.

Although instances of ethical mischief (kickbacks and bribery, insider trading, etc.) might be found in any organization in almost any society, issues such as employee rights, discrimination, and sexual harassment usually create ethical moral mazes for organizations when its managers have to interface with diversity. Subsequently, emphasis in this chapter is placed on assessing the moral mazes that confront organizations within the context of diversity. Particular emphasis is placed on the exploration of three interrelated questions:

- What are the current/future implications of diversity for the ethical practices of U.S. business?
- Do existing ethics-related theories sufficiently address these implications?
- What direction should future research take to advance existing ethics-related theories and practice vis-à-vis diversity.

This chapter begins by first considering some of the macro moral mazes that test the ethical practice of business within the context of diversity. The focus here is on organizations' moral obligation to behave ethically toward their diverse customer base. The ethics-related concepts we are concerned with include social responsibility and social responsiveness. A subsequent section considers micro moral mazes that confront individuals in a diverse workforce. Discussions and recommendations related to the adequacy of current ethics-related theories as they relate to diversity are then presented. The chapter concludes with discussions related to future challenges that organizations and managers will face and have to contend with as they seek to better understand the ethics-diversity relationship.

◪ BUSINESS SOCIAL RESPONSIBILITY TO DIVERSITY

Social responsibility generally refers to those management philosophies, policies, procedures, and actions that have the advancement of society's welfare as one of their primary objectives. The second term in this concept (i.e., responsibility) is fundamentally a moral one that implies an obligation to someone or something—in this case, the obligation is to society. Thus social responsibility can be considered a macro moral maze that organizations will have to navigate as diversity increasingly becomes an issue in American society. Consider the following business behaviors, all having social responsibility implications, as they relate to diversity:

- Cisco, a fortified wine with a 20% alcohol content, aimed at the young adult market. A decision was made by the company to position this product with wine coolers, a product with only a 4%-5% alcohol content.
- Dakota cigarettes, aimed at blue-collar white women who only have a high school diploma and like to attend tractor pull events.
- Player cigarettes, aimed at black males to appeal to the stereotypical image of them as "street smart."
- Nike, L.A. Gear, and other sports footwear companies that use high-profile sports figures in their advertisements to increase sales of high-priced shoes to adolescents who cannot really afford to buy them.
- Companies that discriminate against women and minorities working in their overseas subsidiaries because the 1964 Civil Rights Act does not provide protection for American citizens working abroad for U.S. companies.
- Companies that discriminate against older, homosexual, and disabled employees and then employ "cover up" tactics (e.g., "doctoring" performance evaluations) to avoid lawsuits.

These behaviors raise the issue of whether U.S. businesses are fulfilling their legal and moral obligation to be socially responsible to their diverse constituents (i.e., young adults, women, ethnic minorities, the aged, and the handicapped).

Companies engaging in such behaviors ultimately do act socially responsible toward these diverse constituents, whether by choice or coercion. The issue, however, is whether they are socially responsive to these particular constituents. The social responsiveness of business, or how well a company responds to societal demands and needs, represents an empirical way of assessing its ethical practices vis-à-vis diversity.

▨ BUSINESS SOCIAL RESPONSIVENESS TO DIVERSITY

According to Frederick (1978), the concept of social responsiveness refers to

> the capacity of a corporation to respond to social pressures. The literal act of responding, or of achieving a generally responsive posture, to society is the focus of corporate social responsiveness. . . . One searches the organization for mechanisms, procedures, arrangements, and behavioral patterns that, taken collectively, would mark the organization as more or less capable of responding to social pressures. (p. 5)

Essentially, there are three stages of social responsiveness that relate to diversity. The first stage requires that organizations become aware of potentially important social issues with ethical implications that they need to respond to and act upon. Once important social issues have been identified, the second stage requires organizations to coordinate their activities in response to the issues. The third stage requires organizations to adopt and institutionalize policies designed to cover the issues.

Whereas social responsibility might be considered more a reactive concept in the sense that external pressure can force organizations to become socially responsible, social responsiveness might be considered a more proactive concept. As an illustrative example, consider G. Heileman Brewing Company's 1991 plan to market a malt liquor called PowerMaster to inner-city residents (Manor, 1991). Ethical issues associated with the plan stemmed from the following observations made by critics of the plan:

- Blacks are far more likely to buy malt liquor than whites.
- Malt liquor drinkers are more likely to have dropped out of high school than people who consume regular beer.
- The unemployed are more likely to drink malt liquor than people with jobs.
- PowerMaster contains 30% more alcohol than other malt liquors.
- The plan called for PowerMaster to be promoted heavily in black neighborhoods, primarily to black men.
- Black men have a 70% higher death rate from cirrhosis of the liver than white men, and among some age groups a kind of throat cancer linked to alcohol is 10 times more common among black men.
- The advertising for PowerMaster sells a false promise of getting power and forgetting all your problems.

The fact that government opposition pressured G. Heileman into dropping its plans for PowerMaster suggests that top management at this company subscribed more to the principle of social responsibility than to the principle of social responsiveness. Business ethicists (e.g., Ackerman & Bauer, 1976) would argue that had top managers at this company subscribed to the principle of social responsiveness they would have first recognized that marketing products with ethical implications to their intended market—blacks, Hispanics, and people without much money—was an important social issue, then coordinated the company's activities in response to the issue, and then adopted company policy to cover related issues.

While this is obviously a case of hindsight, current practices in the telemarketing and cognate industries may turn out to be a test case of how well organizations adhere to the principle of social responsiveness vis-à-vis diversity. The ethical implication is that a third of the telemarketing new business is coming from culturally diverse markets. It has been estimated, for instance, that racially, ethnic, and culturally diverse markets are the fastest growing segments of the $500 billion telemarketing business (Byrnes, 1995). Although actions taken by the Federal Trade Commission (FTC) provides some protection (to consumers comprising these market segments) against the unethical practices of some telemarketers, it is the cognate industries (e.g., telecommunications) that must be monitored to assess the extent of their social responsiveness.

For example, companies such as MCI Communications Corporation, Sprint Corporation, and AT&T are deriving a growing percentage of their revenues from telemarketing growth in ethnic, non-English-speaking markets

(Byrnes, 1995). Ethical implications arise from the fact that these mostly immigrant consumers are not always familiar with the products or services being marketed. That makes foreign-language calls longer, and thus more expensive, than calls to English-speaking customers. Whereas some might view this as an unfortunate circumstance associated with a perfectly legal business practice, others might view the practice as an unethical way of increasing profits at the expense of those who are "linguistically challenged."

▧ MACRO SOLUTIONS

Will top management in these telecommunications companies recognize this as a potentially important social issue with ethical implications? Will it (top management) coordinate company activities in response to the issue? Will company policy be adopted to cover this and related issues? If not, the possibility of intervention by the government or interest groups may have financial or other consequences for these and other companies that are not socially responsive to issues that have ethics-diversity implications. The G. Heileman example represented a clear case where government intervention resulted in financial consequences—the company lost its substantial investment in the proposed program.

With respect to interest group intervention, there are some who view the composition of corporate boards that do not reflect diversity of experience, gender, race, and age as an ethic-related issue. Representing one such group is New York's Interfaith Center on Corporate Responsibility. Recently, this group made demands on Microsoft, Chris-Craft, Church & Dwight, and 13 other companies to set a timetable for putting women and ethnic minorities on their corporate board of directors (McMenamin, 1995). Consequences of noncompliance are potential loss of large investments or being forced to put the issue on proxy statements. Although adhering to the principle of social responsiveness would obviate the need for companies to face such consequences, making structural adjustments in their posture toward ethics-diversity issues would facilitate response time. A starting point would be to incorporate ethics-diversity issues throughout the future activity focus of the company. On the diversity side of the issue, activities might entail the following:

- Developing an organizational vision of the ethics-diversity interface that is reflected in the corporate mission statement and integrated throughout business objectives
- Developing a strategic plan for achieving a balance between ethics-diversity issues
- Implementing a process of periodic evaluation for measuring success toward achieving this balance

On the ethics side of the issue, the following five principles of ethical power for organizations espoused by Kenneth Blanchard and Norman Vincent Peale (1988, p. 79) are appropriate:

1. *Purpose*—The mission of our organization is communicated from the top. Our organization is guided by the values, hopes and a vision that helps us to determine what is acceptable and unacceptable behavior.
2. *Pride*—We feel proud of ourselves and of our organization. We know that when we feel this way, we can resist temptations to behave unethically.
3. *Patience*—We believe that holding to our ethical values will lead us to success in the long term. This involves maintaining a balance between obtaining results and caring how we achieve these results.
4. *Persistence*—We have a commitment to live by ethical principles. We are committed to our commitment. We make sure our actions are consistent with our purpose.
5. *Perspective*—Our managers and employees take time to pause and reflect, take stock of where we are, evaluate where we are going, and determine how we are going to get there.

▧ MICRO SOLUTIONS

Whereas macro solutions to ethics-diversity moral mazes focus on action to be taken at the organizational level in response to increasing diversity in U.S. society at large, micro solutions are relevant to ethics-diversity issues in the workplace. Moral issues that micro solutions are most relevant to are diversity-related issues like sexual harassment and discrimination. Micro solutions are aimed at achieving balance between ethics-diversity issues, a task that is the shared responsibility of every individual in the organization. Coleman (1994) set forth some guidelines for the type of responsible behavior that facilitates achieving this balance. The main thrust of these guidelines is that individual behavior acknowledged to be demeaning or offensive, such as racial slurs, race and gender jokes, and sexually suggestive comments or gestures, must change to improve respect and build trust. One might conclude from this thrust that all employees must recognize the impact of their behavior on the organization's efforts toward achieving an ethics-diversity balance.

If this individual-responsibility behavioral change is related to the five principles of ethical power listed in the preceding section on macro solutions, the five principles might be modified as follows for individual employees:

1. *Purpose*—Despite the effects of diversity on my organization's ethical values, I will still view myself as being an ethically sound individual.
2. *Pride*—A balanced self-esteem will keep any negative attitudes I might hold toward diversity from influencing my decisions to engage in unethical behaviors toward diverse individuals.
3. *Patience*—I believe an ethics-diversity balance will eventually be achieved in my company.
4. *Persistence*—My ethical intentions will translate into ethical behavior toward diverse individuals.
5. *Perspective*—I will take time to pause and reflect on my individual responsibility toward helping my organization achieve an ethics-diversity balance.

These modified principles might represent a summary of micro solutions to the moral mazes that individual employees will likely encounter as they become participants in a highly diverse workforce.

◩ PRESENT THEORIES AND FUTURE DIRECTIONS

At the beginning of this chapter the question was asked whether existing ethics-related theories sufficiently address the current and future implications of diversity for the ethical practices of U.S. business. The "normative" approach to ethics appears to sufficiently address this situation. Normative ethics represents a set of principles and standards that would be best for managers to follow within the context of diversity and specifies as well as clarifies the obligation of all organizational participants toward diversity in the workplace. The issue, however, is whether organizations will subscribe to this approach to enhance their ethical posture toward diversity.

Another question asked at the beginning of this chapter was what direction should future research take to advance existing ethics-related theories and practice vis-à-vis diversity? In response to this question, the focus should be more on understanding why existing theories may or may not be used to enhance organizations' posture toward diversity rather than expanding on these theories. Focus might be directed toward changing existing attitudes and thoughts about factors that are important to individuals from all societies, who may eventually find their way into U.S. organizations, and not just those factors considered important in Western societies.

On the one hand, business ethicists suggest that existing (normative) theories can provide a foundation for the continuing managerial concerns about responding to social issues (diversity) in an effective manner. On the other hand, they argue that managerial activities must be based on ethical principles that are acceptable in society at large and consistent with notions of human welfare and fulfillment that are important in Western societies. The question elicited, when diversity is considered, might be: What about Eastern societies? Statistics provided in this book clearly indicate that a preponderance of the increase in U.S. organizations' diversity will come from Eastern societies. In terms of future research directions, then, the focus might be not only on how existing ethics-related theories can and ought to be applied within the context of diversity but finding ways of incorporating multisocietal factors into an organization's basic framework.

◪ FUTURE CHALLENGES FOR MANAGEMENT

What I have attempted to do in this book is give you some idea of the challenges that lie ahead of us as we try to make sense of and manage the ethics-diversity relationship. It is important that we understand the complexities of diversity and the implications that increasing diversity might hold for business and personal ethics. Hopefully, the narrative journey that you have just taken has given you some insights into the nature of the ethics-diversity relationship. Be aware, though, that this relationship is not static. Changing attitudes toward diversity, changing ethical standards, court rulings, and a host of other factors will dictate the nature of this relationship at any given point in time.

For example, a survey of 1,418 U.S. citizens suggested that some segments of American society are calling for an end or at least a slowdown in immigration ("America's Welcome Mat," 1992). This survey indicated that 62% of non-blacks and 47% of blacks in this country would like to see fewer immigrants admitted to the United States. California's Proposition 187, which would restrict illegal immigrants from receiving state benefits, is another indication of growing opposition to immigration. Decreases in immigration would have an impact on the number and types of different cultures and ethnic groups entering U.S. organizations and thus influence the nature and impact of diversity on organizations' ethics paradigms. The challenge for management will be to understand how these changing attitudes will affect the way organizations interface with a possibly new configuration of diversity in both their consumer markets and their workforce.

The U.S. Supreme Court's refusal to review a controversial affirmative action case out of Texas will also create ethical challenges for managers. In the case, known as *Hopwood v. Texas,* the University of Texas law school asked the Supreme Court to uphold its efforts to achieve classroom diversity (Epstein, 1996). Early in 1996, a federal appeals court ruled that it is unconstitutional for the school to consider race in deciding which students to admit and struck down the school's affirmative action plan. The Supreme Court's refusal to review the case is tantamount to upholding the lower court's ruling which, according to constitutional lawyers (e.g., Toobin, 1996), will mean the end of affirmative action.

Implications for business are certain to stem from these legal developments. Indeed, Supreme Court Justice Sandra Day O'Connor has already suggested that she will oppose affirmative action in employment settings. The ethical challenge for managers is whether they will "do the right thing" with regard to hiring, firing, promoting, and behaving ethically within the context of diversity, with no threat of government sanctions to enforce affirmative action.

These two developments (i.e., waning support for immigration and the imminent demise of affirmation action) should give you a feel for the possible ethics-diversity challenges facing management and organizations in the future.

Although not insurmountable, these challenges cannot be met if managers are not adequately equipped to deal with them. This book was not only designed to equip you with an awareness of the possible ethics-diversity challenges facing organizations and managers as we move into the 21st century but also to equip you with some practical ways of thinking about and dealing with these challenges. The cases in Part II provide an opportunity to determine how prepared you are to meet these challenges.

PART II

Cases in Ethics and Diversity

Before you answer the discussion questions at the end of each case, it is recommended that you review the concepts discussed in Chapter 2. Because all of the cases involve ethics-diversity situations within the context of organization and management, reviewing the material in Chapter 6 also will be helpful. As you answer the DISCUSSION QUESTIONS, refer to the following list as a guide to the main concepts covered in the case. Your responses to the DISCUSSION QUESTIONS should incorporate these concepts.

Case	Concepts Covered
Downsizing at Simtek	Role relativism, distributive and procedural justice, rights, managerial values
Chinese Values in American Society	Cultural relativism, individual relativism, values
The Decision to Terminate Randy Shutz	Distributive and procedural justice, rights
Performance Evaluation at Montana Trust & Savings Bank	Managerial and individual values, role, individual, and cultural relativism
Religious Warfare at Jones Consultants	Cultural values, distributive and procedural justice, rights, cultural relativism
Reconciling Diversity and Team Productivity at MSI-Tech	Utilitarianism, managerial values, rights, social responsibility
Hiring Decision at Medcom	Individual values, distributive and procedural justice, rights
Trouble on the Loading Dock	Role relativism, managerial values, distributive and procedural justice, rights
Mark's Dilemma	Distributive and procedural justice, rights, managerial and individual values
Joe Foster's Rules	Distributive and procedural justice, rights, managerial and individual values

NOTE: Case studies are used by permission of the authors.

CASE #1: DOWNSIZING AT SIMTEK

by Shirley A. Hopkins

Karen Jacobs-McKinney is the manager of a group of 10 sales representatives for Simtek, a large computer components manufacturer. The company was founded by President and CEO John Simmons, and has grown from a small privately held start-up company to a large publicly held corporation.

Simtek has been known for fair treatment of its non-union employees and for employee relations policies that are above average. Pay and benefits are in the top fourth of the industry. The only major criticism leveled at Simtek was a charge that the company was not committed to its stated pro-diversity policy. Of its 400 employees, women and minorities represent less than 2%.

Karen Jacobs-McKinney was the first woman of color hired by Simtek and is the only female manager in the company. She has been employed for five years and has worked very hard to be recognized as a fair and capable manager in a white-male-dominated organization. Karen has just been faced with an extremely difficult task. Her immediate superior has told her that Simtek is reengineering and her unit will have to downsize by two or three people. There will be a moderate severance package. Karen has three to four weeks to decide who will be released. Karen has both flexibility and responsibility for selecting among employees that have roughly equal work histories, skills, and potential. She is not happy about the decision but accepts that responsibility as part of her managerial tasks. Karen has been told that she may tell employees about the situation when she is ready.

The Decision

Ms. Jacobs-McKinney is faced with a significant decision that may have multifaceted impacts on her career with the company. The employees in her unit consist of seven white males, one white female, one African American male, and one Asian American female. When she compares the work performance of the 10 she finds that all have performed equally well. All have similar knowledge of the products, and their sales levels are also very similar. Karen must decide on what criteria she will base her decision.

The white males at Simtek have been complaining that the new push toward diversity has caused Simtek to hire almost exclusively women and minorities for the past two years in response to criticism leveled at the company for the lack of commitment to diversity. There has been some talk of a lawsuit claiming reverse discrimination in hiring practices to halt the current hiring trend that favors women and minorities. Within Karen's unit the white female, the African American male, and the Asian American female have all been hired in the past two years in an effort to increase diversity within the organization. The white males have all been employed there at least five years.

Karen is faced with first trying to find a fair criteria for deciding who will be terminated and then how and when to notify the employees of the downsizing. Because all the employees rank approximately the same on job performance, she must consider criteria such as seniority, which will certainly result in at least two of the three newest employees being terminated. These most recent employees are the two women, and the African American man. If two or three of these employees are terminated, then the department will lose all of the diversity that the company has tried to increase in the last two years. Ms. Jacobs-McKinney also knows that if she decides to keep any of the newer employees, then most likely she will be involved with the company in a reverse discrimination suit.

If this wasn't a difficult decision by itself, Karen is also faced with deciding on the timing of the announcement of the downsizing. She is afraid that if she tells the employees early she will lose some of her best employees and that if she waits until the employees are terminated there may be some ethical issues with not giving the employees sufficient warning of the termination. Furthermore, with the tensions rising in the company over reverse discrimination, she fears for her physical safety. Karen must make a decision soon. The personnel manager has just called her requesting the names of the employees who will be terminated. She has one week to decide what to do.

◪ DISCUSSION QUESTIONS

Ethics-Related Questions

1. What ethical issues arise if Karen decides not to give her employees advance warning of the impending downsizing?

2. If the three minority employees are terminated, would this represent any ethical violations on the part of the company or Karen?

3. What type of ethical issues might arise from the charges of reverse discrimination at Simtek?

HRM-Related Questions

1. What criteria do you think Karen should use to decide who will be terminated?

2. What are some motivational/leadership issues that must be considered if Karen decides to give her employees advanced warning of the impending downsizing?

3. Do you think Ms. Jacobs-McKinney has a legitimate fear about her safety? Do you think it has anything to do with her minority status?

CASE #2: CHINESE VALUES IN AMERICAN SOCIETY

by Winter Nie

On most Sunday afternoons, especially when the weather is as nice as it is on this particular Sunday, one would find Chung Kui working in his beautiful flower garden. Today, however, Chung Kui is sitting in front of the television and staring pensively at the telephone. An earlier call from his brother-in-law, Wang Lee, had disturbed his usual peaceful Sunday afternoon. Wang Lee had asked Chung Kui if he could use the work station in his office for a couple of hours because the computers at the university (where he was a Ph.D. student in computer science) were either occupied or down.

Wang Lee's Dilemma

The next day, Monday morning, Wang Lee was expected to turn in a major computer programming project to his advising professor. He actually finished the project on Friday, but on Sunday afternoon he discovered that he had made several programming errors and needed to rewrite most of the program and then rerun it. When he arrived at the campus computer lab, it was packed with students who also had projects due on Monday. When he inquired of the students how long they expected to be using the computers, all of them replied that they would be there until the lab closed. Wang Lee immediately thought of his brother-in-law. He knew that Chung Kui had access to the type of workstation and software required to correct the program and that he could probably get it done faster because his computer was more technologically advanced than the ones at the university computer lab, so he called Chung Kui to ask him for this favor.

Chung Kui's Dilemma

Chung Kui came to America six years ago to work toward a Ph.D. in computer science. After completing his degree, he started a job as a senior programmer for a high-tech computer firm. On Chung Kui's first day at work, his supervisor explicitly explained the company's policy to him. Since it was a high-tech firm that handled defense contracts, security was very important. Individuals other than company employees need authorization from a manager or a supervisor before entering the plant. Computers and software were to be used strictly for company business. Chung Kui was asked to sign his name to indicate that he had read and understood these policies.

Cultural Ties

The friendship between Wang Lee and Chung Kui began years ago when they were college students in China. They used to help each other with assignments and became very close friends. Eventually, Wang Lee met and married Chung Kui's sister. Although he has only been in the United States for less than a year and has had to overcome several language and cultural obstacles, he has been reluctant to ask Chung Kui for help.

When Wang Lee called Chung Kui asking for help, there was very little question whether or not he would provide the help he needed. There were cultural ties that obligated him to help, most notable that he was a relative. In Chinese culture, friendship, family ties, and helping each other are extremely important values that one must respect. So why was he so disturbed when his brother-in-law called him for help? Rather than immediately offering to let Wang Lee use the computer in his office, Chung Kui told his brother-in-law that he was gardening at this moment and could not talk. He promised to call him back in 10 minutes.

▨ DISCUSSION QUESTIONS

Ethics-Related Questions

1. What ethical issues might arise if Chung Kui decides to let his brother-in-law use the company's workstation?

2. How might Chung Kui resolve the conflict between his cultural obligation to his brother-in-law and the ethical obligations he has to his company?

HRM-Related Questions

1. Suppose Chung Kui decides to let his brother-in-law use his computer and management finds out about it? Should the fact that Chung Kui comes from another culture be considered if management decides to discipline him?

2. Should a company's policies be flexible enough to accommodate cultural value differences in a diverse workforce?

CASE #3: THE DECISION
TO TERMINATE RANDY SHUTZ

by Willie E. Hopkins

"We should have never allowed the situation to go on this long. It was a mistake to let Randy complete his probationary period, and we only compounded the problem by transferring him from department to department. Randy should have been told years ago that his performance was marginal, and if he couldn't improve we should have fired him long ago. He was a marginal employee when we hired him 19 years ago and has been nothing but dead wood for the past several years."

So went the discussion at a meeting called to decide whether Randy Shutz, a 58-year-old machine operator, should be terminated. Present at the meeting were Chris Johnson, Randy's current supervisor; Matt Cravens, Chris's manager; and Joe Stearns, the company's personnel manager. After reviewing Randy's personnel file and considering Chris's personal evaluation of Randy, the three concluded that Randy does not have the technical or interpersonal skills needed to succeed in the changing work environment, nor has he been responsive to efforts to improve his skill base.

Since Randy joined Chris's department, he has been assigned routine or "makeshift" tasks. His performance on these tasks has consistently been rated "meets normal requirements," but Randy's value to the department is far below normal. He appears to lack both the ability and the motivation to perform the duties that other machine operators are expected to perform.

Chris explained to Matt and Joe that he has exerted considerable effort during the past six months overseeing the supervision and evaluation of Randy's performance. During this period, Chris evaluated Randy on two occasions as "failing to meet minimum requirements" in three of the five performance criteria. Following the second evaluation, Randy's salary was reduced for a three-month period. This was the only disciplinary action that Randy had received in his 19-year career with the company.

125

After thoroughly discussing the situation, Joe assured Chris and Matt that the department was in a position to proceed with a dismissal action if they decided that was the appropriate action to take. Chris and Matt pondered the question of whether they really wanted to terminate an employee who had been with the company for 19 years, especially when they both agreed that Randy, partly because of his age, would have a hard time finding employment elsewhere. The three of them considered several questions related to their pending decision. The first concerned whether it was ethical to disregard 19 years of "satisfactory" service and whether the department should continue to work with Randy to improve his performance. The other two questions concerned ethical and legal issues associated with Randy's age and his proximity to retirement (he would be eligible for retirement after 20 years of service with the company).

On the other side of the issue was the concern that additional company funds should not be wasted on paying wages to an employee who, during his prime years with the company, was only a marginal performer. Chris also factored in the considerable amount of time and energy he has already expended documenting Randy's performance and arrived at the conclusion that further efforts to salvage this employee would only fail. Joe also noted that he has looked for positions to demote Randy to, but Randy's reputation precedes him and no other managers are willing to accept him in their departments.

◩ DISCUSSION QUESTIONS

Ethics-Related Questions

1. Is it ethical to terminate a long-term employee based on short-term documentation of inadequate performance?

2. What are the ethical and legal implications of terminating Randy, given his age and proximity to retirement?

3. If there are ethical concerns to be dealt with, concerning Randy's possible termination, how should these concerns be balanced against the company's expectation of "acceptable" levels of employee performance?

HRM-Related Questions

1. Are there any reasonable alternatives to terminating Randy?

2. How might management at the company be partly responsible for Randy's poor performance?

3. Are there perhaps some leadership techniques that might be employed to motivate Randy to perform better, or do you feel that such an effort would be a waste of time considering his inadequate skill level?

CASE #4: PERFORMANCE EVALUATION
AT MONTANA TRUST & SAVINGS BANK

by Shirley A. Hopkins

Dottie Johnson had been an operations officer at Montana Trust & Savings Bank for over 10 years, and this time of year never got any easier. It was the policy of the bank for all managers to evaluate their staff at least once per year, and that time had arrived. Dottie always found it difficult to put down on paper her view of an employee's performance. It was inevitable that the employees viewed their performance in a different light than she did. This year was especially hard because she had a fairly new employee who created some real conflict within Dottie. The employee was named Elena Alvarado.

Elena had started working for Dottie just over one year ago. She was a very quiet woman who had recently immigrated to the United States from El Salvador. Dottie found it difficult to talk to her. Elena always seemed so withdrawn and did not freely volunteer information about herself and her family. Dottie knew that she lived with her parents, her young son, and a sister. Other than that she really didn't know any other facts about Elena. Dottie didn't press the matter since she thought Elena had probably experienced some difficult and dangerous encounters with the authorities in her country.

Dottie's dilemma arose from the fact that Elena's performance was excellent in some areas and very unacceptable in others. Dottie had talked with Elena several times during the past year about her performance, telling her that she was a very hard worker and seemed to take well to the details involved in the transactions she processed but that she needed to show more initiative and take on jobs without always waiting for tasks to be assigned her. However, the real problem was that Elena was always calling in sick and often took too much time on her lunch breaks. Elena had missed 32 days in the past year for illness. Dottie had finally resorted to asking her to bring a doctor's note. Dottie hated to do that because it seemed like something that you would ask a child to do in elementary school, not an adult. Elena had promised that she would, but the handwritten notes that Dottie received were obviously not written by a physician. The president of the bank had been informed about the situation and had left it up to Dottie to decide whether Elena should be terminated. Dottie sat at her desk looking at the blank evaluation form.

Elena Alvarado

Elena Alvarado had immigrated to the United States about two years ago. She had worked very hard to save enough money to pay passage for herself, her parents, her son, and her sister to be smuggled into the country. When Elena and her family arrived in Miami they were caught by the immigration and naturalization officers and were supposed to be deported. Elena had met a Catholic priest who helped them file papers and stay in the United States as political exiles. Elena and her father had been kidnapped and beaten by the death squads in El Salvador. Her father had been a government official, and the family felt that it was not safe for them to stay in El Salvador. Elena had attended school at the convent near her home and she was fairly fluent in English. No one else in her family could speak English. Elena was a very good daughter and felt obligated to help her family whenever possible. Her family was everything to her.

When her family had finally been allowed to stay in the United States, Elena decided to find a job similar to the one she had had in El Salvador, that of a bank manager in San Salvador. Yet when she applied for jobs in Miami and mentioned her management experience, all of the bank personnel managers told her there were no management positions open. Elena felt that the people she had talked to were really concerned that she was an immigrant and could not speak English as perfectly as they thought she should instead of evaluating her work experience. Then, Elena received a phone call from Father Brian, the priest who had helped her stay in the country, who told Elena that he knew a friend in the personnel department at a bank in his hometown of Missoula, Montana. Elena did not know where Montana was located, but she decided to move there because she would be able to find work. Elena and her family had been living off the money they had saved in El Salvador, but that was almost gone. With Father Brian's help, she and her family moved to Missoula. Prior to doing so, Elena had flown to Missoula for the interview, and the personnel manager had offered her a job as a foreign exchange teller. It was not a management position, but she was told that if she performed well they would be willing to consider her for promotion when a management position opened.

Elena had worked very hard at Montana Trust & Savings Bank, but she ran into a problem she had not expected. In Miami, there were a lot of Spanish-speaking friends who could help Elena's parents and sister when she was not available to translate for them. In Missoula, Elena did not find anyone else who was fluent in Spanish to help her family communicate when they needed any type of business taken care of. Elena was torn between trying to do her job well and helping her family. Elena had been raised to put her family first in everything, so she began to call in sick when any of the family required a translator. Her parents and her sister were taking English classes, but they found this new language difficult to learn. Elena knew that in time they would be able to learn English well enough that they would not need her to help them, but for now she must be there for them. When Dottie began to talk to Elena about her illnesses, she knew there was a problem.

Dottie had finally asked Elena to provide doctors' notes when she called in sick. Elena didn't know what to do. She thought about telling Dottie about the need to translate for her family, but she had learned very quickly that Americans were not patient with immigrants who did not learn English quickly. Elena was embarrassed to tell Dottie that her family was having a problem learning English. Elena finally decided that she would write a doctor's note for herself. She knew this was not right, but she had seen a doctor's note once at her son's school, and she hoped that Dottie would accept the note without questions. Elena took the note to Dottie, and because Dottie did not say anything to her, she felt everything must be fine. Elena worked extra hard trying to do her job better than any of the other tellers, and she was sure that this would make up for her calling in sick. Elena knew that her performance evaluation was due, and she waited anxiously for Dottie's evaluation of her work. Perhaps she would receive a nice raise and maybe even a recommendation for promotion. Elena had an appointment with Dottie the next morning.

▨ DISCUSSION QUESTIONS

Ethics-Related Questions

1. What should Dottie do concerning Elena's evaluation? What ethical issues arise?

2. How would you have handled the forged doctors' notes. What ethical issues does this raise?

3. If Dottie had been more familiar with Elena's country, language, and customs, do you think she would be in a different position concerning the performance evaluation? How would this affect the ethical issues in this case?

HRM-Related Questions

1. What should Dottie have done to avoid the dilemma she now faces concerning Elena's evaluation?

2. What should you do as a manager when you are unfamiliar with a foreign employee's country, language, and customs? Did Dottie do any of these things?

by Shirley A. Hopkins

Karen Jackson had just finished her performance evaluation for her best systems programmer, Ali Nazari. He had been working for Karen for the past five years. Ali was always very conscientious and hard-working. Karen could never remember a time when Ali did not cooperate with whatever was needed to get the job done. He had postponed his vacations, worked nights, whatever it took. Karen didn't know what she would do without him. She was trying to decide how to tell him that his work hours were going to be changed so that he could work on this new account. Karen knew that this change would last two to three years, for it was the largest contract that Jones Consulting had ever had. Ali was the only person with enough experience to do the programming on this huge job. Karen called Ali on the phone and asked him to meet with her at 2 p.m. today. He told her he would be there.

The Company

Jones Consultants was a small, privately owned consulting firm that specialized in producing custom software for its clients. The firm had a reputation for quality, reliability, and the flexibility to meet its customers' needs. Jones had a small staff of 15 very gifted individuals. Most of the staff consisted of various types of programmers and systems analysts with two managers. This did not include the owner Sophia Jones, who was a systems engineer. Her bachelor's degree was from MIT in computer science, she had an MBA from Harvard, and a Ph.D. in computer science from Carnegie-Mellon. Ms. Jones had worked for a variety of companies and a few consulting companies before starting her own business. Jones Consultants had been in business for 10 years and had been very successful. Each of the employees was valuable to the company in his or her special area of expertise, and all the employees worked together as a team. Ms. Jones felt very fortunate to have so many gifted individuals on her team. She was concerned with harmony and keeping everyone happy. Ms. Jones had just landed a huge $10 million contract to develop a system for a large high-tech manufacturing company. Ms. Jones knew that her staff would be critical in completing this contract on time and within the cost guidelines specified in the contract. Ms. Jones called Karen Jackson on the phone and asked her to come into her office. Karen Jackson was the manager responsible for all the programmers.

Employee Morale

Ms. Jones asked Karen to sit down. Karen was wondering why Ms. Jones had called her into her office. She didn't have to wait long for the answer. Ms. Jones began to tell Karen how important the employees would be in fulfilling the new contract. Karen said that she understood that and asked how she could help. Ms. Jones told her that she wanted her to be as flexible as possible with the employees because they would have to work some strange hours. Ms. Jones explained that to complete the system they had to work around some critical activities at the company so their work would not be disrupted. This meant that her employees would have to tailor their work hours around the needs of the client company. Karen said that she had already been contacted by the client and knew that several of her staff would need to change their work hours to accommodate the client's needs. She also said that she was meeting with one of the key programmers this afternoon. Ms. Jones said that she was glad that Karen was on top of the situation. Karen then stood up and excused herself.

Ali Nazari

Ali had immigrated to the United States six years ago from Iran. He had a bachelor's degree in computer science from a university in Iran and a master's degree from the University of Colorado. He had started work in systems programming in Iran and had immigrated when the political stability of his country began to break down. He was an experienced systems programmer who loved his work. Ali was also an orthodox Sunni Muslim. He took his religion very seriously and was considered a very devout man. Ali never missed his prayer time and was saving money to take a pilgrimage to the holy city of Mecca. He made sure that he prayed three times during the time from dawn to dusk. To minimize conflicts with his work, he prayed first thing when he got up, during his lunch break, and as soon as he got off work. It took about 30 minutes when he knew he was pressed for time. On the weekends, he was able to take longer and pray the traditional five times per day. He felt that it was necessary for him to pray three times during the dawn-to-dusk period to maintain his relationship with Allah. Ali had learned soon after coming to the United States that if he expected to satisfy his employers he had to limit his prayers to three times rather than the traditional five times per day. This accommodation enabled him to minimize any conflict with his work hours and still maintain a relationship with Allah. He knew many Muslims who had fallen away from the faith when they immigrated, but he did not want that to happen to him. He valued his job, but his faith came first.

The Meeting

At 2 p.m. sharp, Ali knocked on the door of Karen's office. He heard her call to him to come in. He opened the door and saw her on the phone. She motioned for him to sit down. Ali came into the office and sat in a chair across from Karen while she finished her conversation and hung up the phone. "Ali I am so glad you could stop by. I know you are busy, but I appreciate your taking the time out. I wanted to give you a copy of your performance evaluation and discuss another matter with you. As you can see, I am very pleased with your work. I have recommended an 8% pay raise for you. I don't really have any negative comments—just keep up the good work. I wanted to talk to you about the new contract." Ali indicated that he had heard about it.

Karen told Ali that he would be crucial to the success of the project. "You are the only systems programmer we have who has the experience to do the work needed for this job. It is a massive project." She also explained that they had to work around the schedule of the client so that their work would not disrupt other activities the client was involved in. Ali said that he knew that and wondered whether there would be more night work. Karen said, "No, not exactly." Ali would need to come into work at 11 a.m. and work straight until 6 p.m. without a break. He would have two hours off and return for another two hours from 8 p.m. until 10 p.m.

Ali immediately thought about his prayer time. He knew that he could pray when he got up and probably pray just before he came to work, but he needed one more prayer time before sunset. It was not appropriate to have the prayer times very close together. He immediately told Karen that his religion required that he have a prayer time before sunset. He told her that he would try to fit in two times before he came to work, but he needed at least 30 minutes some time between approximately 2 and 4 p.m. to complete his other prayers. Ms. Jackson told him that this would cause problems with their client. This was right during the optimal time for the client, but she would try to work it out. Ali made it very clear that he had to have this time off or he might not be able to work on this contract. Karen told Ali that she would be in touch very soon. After he left, Karen knew that she had to do something. She had to have Ali on this project or Jones Consultants might lose the contract. No one else had his expertise. Karen called Ms. Jones and explained the problem. Ms. Jones gave her the name of a contact person at the client's office and Karen placed a call right away. The contact person was out of the office, so she left a message.

The Compromise

Karen received a phone call from the contact person the next morning. She explained the problem, but the contact person was not overly sympathetic, stating that if they made this accommodation it had to be the only one. Any others would disrupt their operations too much. The person told Karen that the other company that Jones Consultants had won the contract from could fully accommodate the client's needs and that any further disruption would throw the contract toward their competitor. Ms. Jackson was very thankful and assured the contact person that there would be no other problems. She hung up the phone and called Ali. She told him that he could have the 30 minutes from 3 to 3:30 p.m. each day that he had to work. She felt good that she was able to save the contract for the company. She knew how much it meant to everyone.

The Issue of Religious Freedom

The next morning Karen received a call from Jeff Guthrie, a software engineer who would also be working on the new contract with Ali. He explained that he heard that Ali was going to receive 30 minutes off between 3 and 3:30 p.m. each day for his prayer time. Jeff had slightly different hours as he would be working on a different part of the client's system. He would be coming in at 10 a.m. and be allowed to take only a 30-minute lunch break from 1:30 to 2 p.m. He explained that he was a devout Christian and met with a Bible study group from 1:30 to 2:30 p.m. three days a week. He told Karen that since Ali was being given time off for prayer he wanted the usual one hour off so he could eat lunch and have his Bible study. He explained that the members of the group could only meet during this time and he felt that he should have this time off. Jeff was a very good employee also, and Karen felt pressure to comply. She explained to Jeff the problem with the client and what she had promised about no further disruptions. Jeff wouldn't give an inch. He said it was a matter of religious freedom. Was Ali's religion more important than his because Jeff was a Christian instead of a Muslim? Karen said, "Of course not," but she just couldn't accommodate him. Jeff said OK and hung up the phone. Karen thought that Jeff had understood. About a week later, Karen received a call from Ms. Jones. She told Karen that she had just been served with papers. The company was being sued by Jeff Guthrie for violation of his religious freedom. Karen was named in the suit. Ms. Jones asked Karen to come to her office immediately.

The Dilemma

When Karen arrived, she was ushered in at once. She began to explain to Ms. Jones about the situation with Ali and the agreement she had made with the contact person at the client company. She also explained what the contact person had said about further disruptions and the possibility of losing the contract. Ms. Jones asked her whether either Ali or Jeff could be replaced. Karen indicated that both had very special skills that would be needed to complete the project. Ms. Jones indicated that she felt Karen should tell Ali and Jeff that religion was not appropriate in the workplace and deny both of them any accommodations. Karen told Ms. Jones that she was sure Ali would quit if he couldn't have his prayer time. Ms. Jones told Karen to think about the situation and make a recommendation to her the next week. Karen left with a feeling of doom settling over her.

▧ DISCUSSION QUESTIONS

Ethics-Related Questions

1. What are some ethical/legal issues that may arise if Ali is allowed prayer time and Jeff is not allowed Bible study time, or vice versa?

2. To your knowledge, are there any ethical/legal issues associated with allowing or disallowing the practice of religious freedom in the workplace? Should there be?

HRM-Related Questions

1. What HRM issues might arise if Karen follows Ms. Jones's advice and denies both Ali's and Jeff's request to practice their religion in the workplace?

2. What would you do if you were in Ms. Jackson's position? What recommendation would you make to Ms. Jones?

CASE #6: RECONCILING DIVERSITY
AND TEAM PRODUCTIVITY AT MSI-TECH

by Shirley A. Hopkins

Jena Davis, a self-professed female entrepreneur, founded Manufacturing Systems Incorporated (MSI) 15 years ago. MSI manufactures sophisticated prototype products for high-tech companies such as IBM, Hewlett-Packard, and Texas Instruments. The types of products manufactured by MSI require a highly technically skilled workforce.

During the past few years, Ms. Davis has opened three subsidiaries of MSI. All three, including the parent company, have been extremely successful. In fact, the company has been so profitable that plans have been made to open up a fourth subsidiary.

Management Philosophy

Ms. Davis's educational background is in engineering. She keeps up with the latest technologies in her industry and has implemented new production techniques such as JIT (just-in-time) and TQM (total quality management). She is a strong believer that the use of techniques such as these will give her company a competitive advantage and will result in improved profitability. Subsequently, she has been very careful to adhere to all the suggested guidelines required to successfully implement these techniques.

Specific guidelines include using teams as a primary method of achieving productivity goals, promoting effective teamwork with these teams, facilitating intra- and interteam communication, and training all team members in the technical aspects of these techniques (e.g., statistical process control).

Impetus for Change

One evening as Ms. Davis was reviewing the plans for the fourth MSI subsidiary, the personnel manager, Mr. Neil Strong, walked into her office and handed her a copy of a book titled *Workforce 2000: Work and Workers for the 21st Century*. Mr. Strong, knowing that Ms. Davis liked to keep abreast of any new developments that might impact her business interests in any way, suggested that she read this book before finalizing the plans for the fourth MSI subsidiary.

The gist of the book was this:

- There is a very high probability that between now and the year 2000, the United States will experience an acute shortage of highly skilled technical workers.
- Since U.S.-born white males will only represent 9%-15% of all new entrants to the labor force, there will not be nearly enough of them to fill the highly technology-oriented jobs that will dominate U.S. industry in the future.
- Subsequently, U.S. companies will have to hire significantly more women, minorities, and foreign nationals to fill the gap.
- The proactive company will begin now to recruit highly skilled and technically trained women, minorities, and foreign nationals and do all it can to retain them.

Workforce Diversity at MSI-Tech

Ms. Davis was deeply concerned about predictions made in the book, so much so that the very next day she instructed Mr. Strong to begin a search for highly qualified women, minorities, and foreign nationals to staff MIS-Tech, the fourth subsidiary being planned. MSI-Tech opened within two years and, like the other MSI subsidiaries, used the latest technologies and employed a highly skilled, technically trained workforce.

However, unlike the other subsidiaries, MSI-Tech's workforce was highly diverse. To ensure diversity, Mr. Strong had recruited a significant number of foreign nationals with experience in high-tech U.S. companies. Although they were highly skilled and technically trained, their proficiency in the English language was low and they did not understand very much about the subtleties and nuances of U.S. culture and work attitudes. Despite these cultural deficiencies, the personnel manager felt that their skill and technical training would overcome any potential cultural-related conflict that might arise. These foreign nationals represented 22% of MSI-Tech's workforce; African Americans,

Mexican Americans, and Asian Americans represented 15%, 13%, and 17%, respectively; and U.S.-born white males and white females represented 12% and 21%, respectively.

Substandard Team Productivity

One year following the opening of MSI-Tech, a comprehensive analysis of its operations was conducted. The analysis was precipitated by preliminary reports that the new subsidiary was not performing as well as the others. A comparison of MSI-Tech's operations with those of the other subsidiaries found that the productivity levels of the various work teams comprising MSI-Tech's workforce were significantly lower than those of teams comprising the workforces at the other subsidiaries. The lower productivity levels at MSI-Tech translated into lower profitability for the whole corporation.

All the workers were highly skilled and technically trained, so why was team productivity lower at MSI-Tech? This was a question that Ms. Davis pondered. She was not accustomed to her subsidiaries performing at substandard levels. She would rather shut down the entire operation at MSI-Tech than have its substandard team productivity affect overall corporate performance. Indeed, this was her intention if causes of the substandard team productivity could not be found and remedied. The next day she called Mr. Strong into her office.

The MSI-Tech Decision

The following conversation took place between Ms. Davis and Mr. Strong:

Ms. Davis: Neil, have you seen the recent productivity statistics for MSI-Tech?

Mr. Strong: Yes, I have, and I'm very concerned.

Ms. Davis: Do you have any idea what might account for the low productivity of the work teams? It's real puzzling, since we've had such good results at all of the other sites.

Mr. Strong: I don't know what could be causing the problem. We screened each of the employees very carefully, and they are all highly skilled, highly motivated individuals. The only difference between MSI-Tech and the other facilities is the degree of cultural diversity.

Ms. Davis: Well, I know it is a hard decision, but I think that we owe it to our stakeholders to close the facility as soon as possible. This was a great experiment that doesn't seem to work. I want you to set up a plan to close the facility by December 15 and begin processing severance notices immediately.

Mr. Strong: That only gives me four weeks to close this facility and lay off the entire workforce. That isn't very much notice for this time of the year. Don't you think we need to take time and look into this problem to see whether there might not be a better solution?

Ms. Davis: Normally I would agree. However, the economy has been showing signs of a downturn, and I don't think we can afford to carry this facility any longer. We are losing money every day that it is open. Another company has been interested in the facility and land. We need to take advantage of these options now. Proceed with the plan and let me know when I can let the other company know that the facility will be available.

◨ DISCUSSION QUESTIONS

Ethics-Related Questions

1. What are some of the ethical and legal issues that MSI might face as a result of the closing of the facility?

2. Does the fact that the facility is staffed primarily with women, ethnic minorities, and foreign nationals raise the ethical considerations of closing the facility to a higher level than if the facility were staffed primarily with white males? Discuss.

HRM-Related Questions

1. What might be some of the possible causes of the low work team productivity at MSI-Tech?

2. What are some possible solutions to the causes you have uncovered?

3. Would you proceed with the closing if you were Mr. Strong? If not, what would you do?

by Shirley A. Hopkins

James Kennedy had just hung up from talking with his best friend Bob Morris. James smiled pleasantly as he remembered all the fun he and Bob had had at Stanford. The four years there were probably the "best" years of his life. James had met Bob during the fraternity rush at the beginning of their freshman year. James had always known that he would go to Stanford, but for Bob it was very difficult. Bob's family had been very poor, and even with financial aid he had to take on extra jobs to make ends meet. James always wondered why Bob had pledged Kappa Epsilon Gamma. The dues and other fees were just one more financial burden he had to carry. James always marveled at Bob's determination to graduate from Stanford and be a Kappa man, too. Over the years, James had seen Bob overcome many obstacles to success. Bob was motivated to surpass his goals in life by as large a margin as possible. He never knew when to call it quits.

The reason why James had called Bob was to tell of an opening for a regional marketing manager at Medcom. James had just been informed that his current regional manager had accepted a promotion in one of Medcom's other divisions. Medcom was primarily a telecommunications company but recently had acquired companies in satellite communication and fiber optics production. It was a rapidly growing company with many exciting opportunities for managers willing to go the "extra mile." James couldn't think of a better person for the job. He was excited about the possibility of being reunited with his old friend. James would have to publish the position opening, but ultimately he would have the authority to hire the new regional manager. James was sure that this would be a steppingstone for Bob within Medcom. He couldn't wait to get home and tell his wife Susan.

The next morning he received an e-mail from Jennings Rydell, president of the company, asking that James meet with him at 11 a.m. today to discuss the regional manager position. James couldn't think of the reason why Mr. Rydell would want to see him. At 11 a.m. James arrived at Mr. Rydell's office. After a few minutes he was ushered in.

Mr. Rydell began by complimenting James on his job as vice president of marketing. He then began to tell James that the Board of Directors had recently indicated to him that Medcom needed to improve its hiring of women and minorities to further its diversity goals. Mr. Rydell then indicated that he wanted James to try very hard to find a qualified female and/or minority candidate for the regional manager position. James indicated that he had a good candidate in mind; however, he was not a minority. Mr. Rydell told James that he wanted him to interview other candidates with an eye toward a woman and/or a minority. James could tell that Mr. Rydell was very serious about this request. James excused himself and returned to his office. He decided to go out for lunch and think about how he would approach this job search.

James had just returned from lunch when the phone rang. It was June Deevers, the personnel manager. June had been contacted by Mr. Rydell, and she told James that she had several good candidates who met Mr. Rydell's diversity goals. She said that she would drop off the applications and resumés in about an hour. Almost immediately the phone rang again. This time it was Bob on the other end, telling James how excited he was about the job and that he was writing his letter of resignation. Bob planned on giving the letter to his manager tomorrow afternoon. James didn't know what to say. He was afraid to tell Bob to stop preparing his resignation as he had more or less promised him the job. Well, maybe the candidates that June had found wouldn't be as qualified as Bob and he could just tell Mr. Rydell that he had made a good effort but Bob was far more qualified than the rest. Yes, he was sure that would be true. He knew Bob's qualifications were excellent. Bob had graduated from Stanford with honors in marketing and had 10 years of marketing experience. Granted it wasn't in telecommunication, but it was good solid industry experience. He decided not to say anything to Bob right now. He wanted to make this happen for his friend who was like a brother to him. He had to make it work. He told Bob he had to cut the call short for a meeting and would get back to him tonight.

June brought the folders in and laid them on James's desk. She told him that there were several really good candidates, especially an African American woman named Tanya Burton-Hughes. June told James that she had taken the liberty of asking Ms. Burton-Hughes to stop by this afternoon. She apologized for doing this without asking James first, but she was sure that a competitor was interested in hiring Ms. Burton-Hughes and she didn't want Medcom to miss the chance to hire such a good prospect. James thanked her for bringing him the folders and said he would get back to her after he'd had a chance to look them over and meet with Ms. Burton-Hughes.

He was almost afraid to open the folders, but he knew that he must. He took the first one and quickly flipped to the resumé. It was an Asian man who had attended Northwestern University. He had majored in finance but had been working in marketing for three years. His work experience was primarily computer companies. James was relieved. Bob was certainly more qualified than this person. He picked up the next folder. This candidate was a Hispanic woman. She also was not as qualified as Bob. He was beginning to feel relieved. He glanced at two other resumés, and they were similar to the first two. Their qualifications were good but not as good as his friend's. One folder was left. This must be the woman that June had mentioned. He took a deep breath and opened it.

Tanya Burton-Hughes had graduated summa cum laude from Harvard Business School with a major in marketing. She had worked in the broadcast industry while in school. After completing her B.S., she had worked for a large telecommunication company in the Boston area and had returned for an MBA at Harvard. Ms. Burton-Hughes had 12 years of experience in telecommunication or related businesses. She had shown a continued pattern of increased responsibility within the companies that she'd worked for. It seemed that the only reason why she left a company was a significant opportunity for continued growth and promotion within the industry. She was indeed impressive. What made it even more difficult was that not only was she female but she was also a minority. How was he going to tell Mr. Rydell that he had selected a white male who was a little less qualified over a highly qualified African American female? James was miserable. He had to decide what to do. He knew that Mr. Rydell would let him hire Bob, but he also knew that there would be future ramifications.

At 2 p.m., James heard his secretary's voice over the intercom telling him that a Ms. Burton-Hughes was waiting to see him. James composed himself and told Jane to show her in. He rose from his chair to greet the young woman who had just entered his office. She was very well dressed, rather thin, with small wire-framed glasses. He introduced himself and asked her to sit down. He asked her why she was interested in Medcom, and she began to relate how

she had worked in the broadcast industry throughout college and upon gradu-
ation had decided to stay in the industry for her career. She liked the challenge
of the telecommunication field with the constantly changing technology. It was
exciting and offered many interesting opportunities. However, she noted that
jobs were getting more scarce due to the current economic downturn. They
talked in a relaxed way about her goals and qualifications for the position that
was opening. James felt at ease with her. He liked Ms. Burton-Hughes very
much. By the time they had finished their meeting, James found himself saying
things he had not expected to say: "I am so glad we had a chance to meet. I find
your qualifications very impressive. I'm sure you will be a perfect match for
what we are looking for in a regional marketing manager." She smiled and
offered her hand as she rose to leave. "I'm sure Medcom will be very lucky to
have you come on board. We'll be in touch very soon," James told her.

He stretched his aching shoulders and began to pack his briefcase to leave.
He had a long commute home and some time to think about all of this before
he called Bob tonight. James had just walked in the door weary from the
dilemma that faced him when he heard the phone ring. He prayed that it
wouldn't be Bob on the phone. He heard Susan laugh and knew it must be Bob.
Bob always said something funny to make Susan laugh when he got her on the
phone. He heard Susan say "Just a minute and I'll get him." Susan came into
the living room where James had collapsed into a chair. She smiled brightly and
said, "Bob is on the phone. Won't it be great to have him and Jenni close by
again?" She saw the frown on James's face, and she knew something was wrong.
"Is there something I can do?" she asked him. James shook his head, and then
he thought for a moment. Maybe if he had some time to discuss it with Susan.
"Susan, could you please tell Bob that I'll call him back in a few minutes? Then
please come back, I need to talk to you." She walked out of the room and gave
Bob the message.

Susan returned to the living room and sat down beside James on the couch.
She knew this look on his face; she knew there was major conflict behind it.
James told her about Mr. Rydell's requests concerning the hiring of a woman
and/or minority for the regional manager's position and about the various
candidates that June Deevers had brought to him for consideration. He told
her about his meeting with Ms. Burton-Hughes and how impressed he was with
her. Susan carefully listened to all that James had to say and then sat quietly for
a few moments. James had always respected Susan's advice. She always seemed
to have a better sense of logic and fairness when hard decisions were faced.

Susan said, "I think you have to offer the job to Tanya. She is by far the most qualified. I think Mr. Rydell would accept Bob if he were truly the best qualified, but he isn't. Maybe another job will open up for Bob." I knew she was right. I had already come to this conclusion, but I also knew how much I wanted Bob to have this opportunity. It would mean that my old friend could be near and advance toward his career goals at the same time. It seemed so perfect for him. I had to hope that Susan was right, that maybe another job would come up. I thanked her for her help and walked into the hallway to call Bob.

I dialed the phone and heard Bob's familiar voice at the other end. Before I could say a thing to him, he began to tell me how his boss that come into his office while he was typing his letter of resignation. He said that he was afraid to let his secretary type it because he was sure someone would see it before he was ready. Imagine, his boss had just casually walked into his office and saw the letter on the computer screen. Well, needless to say, he had to tender his resignation on the spot. His boss had told him that it would be effective immediately. "So I sure hope that the job is set, because we will be moving sooner than we had planned."

James listened with his mouth open. He was stunned. Bob was out of a job. Why hadn't he told him earlier to stop writing the letter? He could have prevented this mess. James didn't know what to say. He couldn't tell him about his decision now. Bob and his family would be left without an income and would probably lose everything he had worked for for 10 years. He knew that even with Bob's experience the job market was pretty tough right now.

For that matter, how would James handle Mr. Rydell? He could find himself in the same situation if he didn't make the right decision. If he hired Bob, he was concerned about how Ms. Burton-Hughes would react when she found out that the job had gone to a white male who was less qualified. There could be possible legal problems for Medcom. He would be in big trouble if that should happen. He told Bob that he was very sorry about what had happened and that he would have things settled about the job in a few days. James could hear the sudden change in Bob's voice: "James, I thought every-thing was settled. I wouldn't have been writing my letter of resignation if I had known there were some loose ends. You can't let me down, buddy. Right?" James told Bob not to worry, that everything would be fine, and he hung up. What in the world was he going to do?

⬚ DISCUSSION QUESTIONS

Ethics-Related Questions

1. What are some organizational-related ethical issues that James must resolve?

2. What are some personal ethical conflicts that James must resolve in his own mind?

3. What ethical mistakes did James make in handling this situation? What would you have done instead?

HRM-Related Questions

1. How could James have avoided the problems with Mr. Rydell? Explain your answer. What should have been done differently?

2. What decision would you make if you were James? Explain your answer.

CASE #8: TROUBLE ON THE LOADING DOCK

by Minnette A. Bumpus, David B. Balkin, and Wilfred J. Lucas

Bob Jackson is the new operations manager of a hospital supply distribution center for a medical supplies corporation. Performance at the distribution center has been declining over the past few months, and Bob accepted this new position knowing that top management expected him to turn around the performance at the distribution center as quickly as possible. He also accepted his new position knowing that corporate headquarters had initiated several diversity initiatives and that his workforce at the distribution center would consist of several members of ethnic minority groups, a strong contingent of women, and several foreign nationals. The rest of his 50-plus employees consisted of white males.

Bob was sitting in his office one afternoon planning some policy changes to improve the efficiency of the distribution center when a supervisor rushed in and told him there was trouble on the loading dock. Two employees, Ed Williams and Buddy Jones, had just gotten into a heated dispute and the situation on the loading dock was very tense.

The Situation

The distribution center had an informal policy that allowed employees to listen to music while they worked. Employees considered having the right to listen to music a benefit that improved their working conditions. However, there is no policy governing the choice of music station selection. Whoever arrived at the center first got to select the station and thus the type of music that would be listened to that day. On this particular day, Ed Williams, a black employee, insisted that he and the other black employees on the loading dock

---

NOTE: This case study was first presented at the 1995 Western Casewriters Association Case Workshop under the title "Administering discipline within the context of diversity."

could not stand to listen to the country-western music that Buddy Jones, a white employee, had selected. Williams insisted that the station be changed. Jones claimed that the rap music that the black employees wanted to listen to was offensive to him and the other white employees and made it difficult for them to work effectively. Jones and Williams got into an emotional and angry argument over the music and began yelling racial slurs at one another.

Bob Jackson's Dilemma

As Bob raced toward the loading dock, he reflected on an article he had recently read titled "Keeping Hate Out of the Workplace." This article predicted an increase in race-related conflicts as the U.S. workplace becomes more diverse. When Bob arrived at the loading dock, he demanded to know what was going on. The loading dock supervisors told Bob that Ed Williams had instigated the fight by violating the "music policy" and then exacerbated the problem by making derogatory remarks about the music preferences of white people. The supervisors also told Bob that Ed has had previous disciplinary problems at the distribution center and recommended that he be terminated at once.

By way of the "grapevine" and personal observations, Bob learned that relationships between the loading dock supervisors and some of the black employees were poor. Knowing this, he considered whether he should act on the advice of the supervisors and terminate Ed Williams or take some other disciplinary action. Considering the severity of the conflict, Bob felt that he needed to take immediate action to resolve this problem and head off a potentially volatile situation.

◤ DISCUSSION QUESTIONS

Ethics-Related Questions

1. What are some potential ethical issues associated with this case?
2. Would Bob Jackson be acting unethical if he decides to take disciplinary action against Ed Williams (a black employee) and not Buddy Jones (a white employee), or vice versa? Explain.

3. Considering the diversity of employees working on the loading dock, does the use of racial slurs constitute unethical behavior?

HRM-Related Questions

1. Could the conflict on the loading dock be a cause of declining perform-ance at the distribution center? If so, what seems to be the "true" cause of the conflict, and what should Bob Jackson do to settle it?

2. What can Bob Jackson do on a more long-term basis to ensure that incidents such as the one described in this case are less likely to occur in the future?

3. What other human resource issues are present in this case, and how might they be resolved?

CASE #9: MARK'S DILEMMA

by Shirley A. Hopkins

Angela Moore sat at her desk thinking about all the things she had to finish before she could leave to meet her husband, Ken, at the Jambalaya Restaurant for dinner. They had reservations for 7 p.m., and it was already 5:45 p.m. She still had the marketing reports to finish and had just heard a fax coming in. She knew Ken would be giving her a frown if he could see her rushing around like this. He had reminded her twice not to be late for her birthday celebration tonight. Ken knew that she worked too hard, and he knew the effect that all that stress had on her body.

As Angela ran to the fax machine, she suddenly was gripped by a horrible feeling of nausea and the room began to spin. She knew she had gone beyond the point of tolerance. Her body was screaming out for some rest. She collapsed on the floor, with the room spinning around and around. She hadn't had a vertigo attack in quite a while, not since she had started her medication two years ago. Prior to this, Angela had had some minor balance episodes but not full-blown vertigo. Her heart sank. She was so glad no one was in the office to see her condition. She knew that if she laid very still for a few minutes it might start to subside. In about 30 minutes the attack was over. She knew that to meet the reservation time now she would have to call a taxi. The work would have to wait until morning. As she dialed the taxi company she thought about how difficult the past few years had been.

Angela's and Ken's Health Problems

Three years ago she had been diagnosed with Meniere's disease, an inner ear disorder that caused tinnitus (ringing or buzzing in the ears), vertigo, and hearing loss. Doctors don't usually know what causes it, and the treatments are really aimed at managing the symptoms. Many people who have Meniere's are totally disabled, but Angela was determined to continue her job as a market

151

analyst for a public utility company. She had been with the company nearly 19 years. She had worked her way up in a predominately male organization and had hopes of being promoted to marketing director before she retired.

Along with her own health problems, Angela's husband had recently been diagnosed with a congenital joint disorder that would eventually cause him to be restricted to a wheelchair. At times, Angela had to help Ken get around. His condition hadn't progressed to the point where their medical insurance would cover some of the types of equipment that would help Ken get around independently. They didn't have enough money to afford this expensive equipment on their own. So they were trying to make do until the medical coverage would assist them. The doctors had no idea when that would be. It could be months or years.

Reasonable Accommodations

Angela had been trying not to let her manager know about all of these personal matters, but after she had to ask for several part days off to help Ken do some things for his job, she finally broke down and told Mr. Kline what was going on. She explained Ken's situation and her medical condition. She felt that he needed to know what she was dealing with so he wouldn't think that she was letting her job go. Angela had always taken pride in her work. She always received outstanding performance evaluations, and she wanted Mr. Kline to know that he could still depend on her. She just had to be creative at times in completing her work.

Angela had a computer at home, so she asked the company to buy a modem for her so she could download information from work and finish her work at home. She could then upload the finished documents and e-mail them to her coworkers. She found that using technology from home really helped her stay on top of her work. Mr. Kline said he thought that was a reasonable accommodation and that he had no problem with her using technology to assist her in completing her work just as long as she was in the office most of the time. Angela assured Mr. Kline that she would be in as much as she could. So everything seemed to be going well. However, work had gotten pretty crazy lately. Ken was getting a little worse, and Angela found that her condition was flaring up more too. She was putting in 10- and 12-hour days trying to get the work done on a new campaign as well as keep track of her other duties. The pressure was building, so it was no wonder she had the vertigo again. She knew she had to back off some, or there would be real problems. How could she help Ken if she was lying in bed with vertigo?

A Promotion Opportunity

She had enjoyed her 55th birthday celebration. Ken had surprised her with a number of her friends arriving at the restaurant when she had only expected Ken. After dinner, she told him about the vertigo. He gave her that worried look that only she understood. He didn't say anything, but she knew that he wanted her to get some rest. Her vacation was coming up in about a month and she really needed it. The next morning when she arrived at work, Mr. Kline asked her to come into the office. He told her that Steve Gage, the marketing director, was being moved to another position within the company. He wanted her to be the first to know. He told her that the chief operating officer would be selecting a new marketing director, and he knew that this had been a goal of hers for some time. Angela thanked Mr. Kline for telling her and asked if he would recommend her for the job. Mr. Kline said that he would be glad to put in a word for her. She smiled and thanked him and then returned to her desk. As soon as she could, she called Ken with the news. Ken was delighted, but then a hesitation came into his voice: "Are you sure you can handle that kind of pressure?" Angela hadn't really thought about that, but after a minute or two she said yes, she could. It would be difficult, but might actually be better because her duties would be different and she would basically be her own boss. She could set her schedule as she liked, as long as she met her obligations. Ken said, "Go for it!"

A Critical Meeting

About a week later, Mark Kline received a call from John Dye, the chief operating officer. He asked Mark if he knew of some good candidates for the marketing director position. Mark said that Angela Moore was a very capable market analyst who would be well suited for the position. Mr. Dye asked Mark to have lunch with him so they could discuss, in more detail, the requirements of the position and how Angela might fit those requirements. Mark said that he would be happy to do that. The lunch meeting took place three days later, during which Mr. Dye told Mark that he wanted a more aggressive approach to marketing than the previous director had supplied. He said that the candidate would have to be a "real go-getter." The public sector was changing, and they had to be proactive if they were going to survive. John Dye asked Mark if Angela fit that profile.

Mark hesitated a little; he wasn't sure what to say. He knew that Angela had confided in him about her and Ken's health problems in hopes that Mark would understand her special needs but not for it to be public knowledge. Mark wasn't sure he should tell Mr. Dye about these matters. Before he could answer, Mr. Dye said, "Oh, by the way, how long did you say Angela has been with the company?" Mark said, "Let me see, I think this is her 18th year." "How close is she to retirement?" Mr. Dye asked. "Well, not for another 10 years." Mr. Dye smiled. "So she's about 55, right?" Mark said yes, since he had heard her talking about her birthday party. Before Mark could say anything else, Mr. Dye received a call on his cell phone. "Sorry, Mark, I'll have to continue this another day. I have a very pressing problem that I must attend to." Mark said that he would be available when Mr. Dye would like to reschedule.

Mark's Dilemma

As Mark walked away he found himself confronted with a real dilemma. He could tell that Angela's age was becoming an issue with Mr. Dye and if he told him about her and Ken's medical problems that would probably eliminate her chances of promotion. He thought that Angela would be great in the job. She was so creative and dedicated. He didn't know of any other employee who would have been able to do the things she had been asked to do under the circumstances and do them so well. He had to decide very soon what and what not to tell Mr. Dye.

▨ DISCUSSION QUESTIONS

Ethics-Related Questions

1. What might be some ethical/legal implications involved with the discussions between Mark and Mr. Dye, particularly the discussion about Angela's age?

2. What legal/moral issues would arise if Angela was eliminated as a candidate for promotion because of her medical problems?

HRM-Related Questions

1. The Americans with Disabilities Act (ADA) requires that employers make reasonable accommodations for employees with disabilities. If Angela is promoted, what other reasonable accommodations might the company make to ensure that she succeeds in her new job?

2. Persons with disabilities are not only protected by the ADA but by Affirmative Action as well. In your opinion, should Angela be given preference for the promotion because she is part of a protected-class group? Discuss and debate.

CASE #10: JOE FOSTER'S RULES

by Shirley A. Hopkins

Kevin Harper had just completed his first year at a large western university. He was majoring in business and had hopes of going on to law school. His ultimate goal was to be a stockbroker on Wall Street and then eventually enter his father's law firm. He was spending his first summer away from home. It was tough, but he was determined not to ask his father for any money this summer. He had to find a job that would cover his expenses until fall arrived along with the tuition checks and allowance from his parents. He hated taking money from them, but they always insisted. Kevin remembered that one of his friends had mentioned that the café where he worked needed some help, so he decided to check it out.

Kevin and Paul's Relationship

Kevin's partner, Paul, was also a business major, and they shared a small apartment together over a pizza restaurant. Kevin had met Paul a week after arriving at school and knew that Paul was the person he had been waiting for all his life. Kevin's parents were aware that he was gay, but they refused to talk about it. Kevin was still uncomfortable with being openly gay, and Paul seemed to understand when Kevin introduced him to his friends as his roommate. Paul had had some very bad experiences with gay bashing in his hometown, so he understood that it was hard to let others know one's sexual preference.

The Daily Grinder

Kevin walked into the Daily Grinder. It was a nice little café, with an old-fashioned, homey atmosphere that served food like meat loaf sandwiches and gravy fries. The college students weren't old enough to remember this kind of food, so it was like they were discovering it for the first time. They loved it.

The café was always packed at lunchtime, and dinnertime was pretty busy too. The owner was a big friendly man named Joe Foster. Joe was known to be a very pious Christian who tried to treat his employees very fairly. However, he made it very clear that he had some strict rules that seemed to be rooted in his religious beliefs. Kevin's friend, Tom, had mentioned this but said that Mr. Foster was a good boss and paid his employees better than most of the restaurants in town. Kevin's friend said that he was sure Kevin wouldn't have any problems with the rules, so Kevin decided that he would give it a try since he really needed the money to get through the summer.

Kevin asked the hostess if he could speak with Mr. Foster. She told Kevin to have a seat at the counter and she would get Joe. Mr. Foster came out of the kitchen with a big apron on. He reached out and shook Kevin's hand and asked him how he could help him. Kevin told Mr. Foster that his friend Tom had told him that there was an opening there and he really needed a job for the summer. Mr. Foster told Kevin that he was having to fill in for the cook today and that he didn't have time to talk. He asked Kevin if he could stop back tomorrow at 3 p.m. Kevin said that he would see him then. As Kevin left he looked around more carefully. He noticed some pictures on the wall with Bible verses and a stack of dove stickers at the cash register. He began to wonder about the "rules" Tom had referred to. He decided not to jump to any conclusions until he had a chance to talk to Mr. Foster.

At 3 p.m. sharp, Kevin walked into the Daily Grinder. Mr. Foster was sitting at a corner booth and motioned for Kevin to come over. He shook Kevin's hand and asked him to have a seat. Joe began to ask Kevin about his work experience and what type of positions he had most recently held. Kevin told Mr. Foster about his summer work as a waiter at the country club back home. He told him that this was his first summer away from home and that he really needed a job. Joe smiled at Kevin. Joe thought that Kevin looked a lot like his nephew; he liked him right away. In spite of Kevin's modest work experience Joe offered him a waiter position on the spot. Kevin was delighted. Joe told him to report for work at 10:30 a.m. the next day to work the lunch shift.

Kevin was walking on air when he opened the apartment door. Paul was starting dinner, and Kevin gave him a hug and told him about the job. Paul asked Kevin whether Mr. Foster had mentioned the rules Tom had told him about, and Kevin said, "No, maybe Tom was just exaggerating." All he knew was that Mr. Foster seemed really nice and was paying Kevin twice what the other restaurants were paying per hour. Also, Tom had told him that at lunchtime the tips were fantastic. Paul was happy for him, and they settled down for a quiet evening watching videos.

The Rules

Kevin arrived at work the next day. Mr. Foster had some papers for him to sign. These were the usual social security and disability types of things. Then he told Kevin that he had some special rules for his employees. He told Kevin that he was a very religious man and that he conducted his business in a godly fashion. He didn't approve of employees dating, he didn't approve of swearing at work, and he didn't approve of any lewd conduct. Kevin asked him how he defined lewd conduct. Joe said, "Oh, you know, wearing low-cut clothes for the female employees, homosexuals, hugging or kissing in the café, things like that." Joe asked Kevin if he had a problem with those types of things. Kevin turned a little red but said no, he didn't. Kevin knew that the chances of Mr. Foster finding out that he was gay were pretty small. Joe said, "Great! I'm real happy to have you working here." Kevin thanked him and went out to get started. Kevin had a busy day, and at the end of his shift he had made over $50 in tips. Tom told him this was pretty typical. Kevin knew that he had made the right decision not telling Mr. Foster that he was gay.

The Encounter

Things went well. Kevin had been working for Joe Foster about a month and a half. Joe had more or less adopted Kevin and had told him how much he reminded him of his favorite nephew. Kevin was happy that he was doing so well. One afternoon just before Kevin got off work, Paul came into the restaurant, sat at the counter, and ordered a cup of coffee and a slice of cherry pie. He was waiting for Kevin to finish his shift so they could go to a movie. When Kevin went into the back to hang up his apron, Joe called him over and asked him about Paul. Kevin said that Paul was his roommate. Joe said good-bye and that he would see him tomorrow. Kevin and Paul walked out and got into the car.

Joe walked out the back door to check on a delivery driver who had just arrived. From around the corner of the truck he saw Kevin give Paul a hug just before they drove away. Joe was shocked and just stood and stared for a while. He couldn't believe what he had just seen.

Kevin arrived at work early the next day. Joe was in the kitchen filling in for the cook who was sick again. Kevin smiled and waved, but he noticed that Joe seemed to be ignoring him. It was this way all day. Kevin wondered what was going on with Joe but thought it was probably due to the cook being out—and it had been a very busy day. This same coolness went on for about a week. At the end of the week, Kevin picked up his pay envelope. Inside was a pink slip. Joe had written a note saying that business was slowing down and he didn't need him any longer. He said he was sorry and had included two weeks' severance pay. Kevin was stunned. He went to Joe and asked him about the pink slip. Joe basically said the same thing he had written in the note. Kevin didn't know what to say. He knew that business wasn't slow, but he didn't know what he had done. Kevin left wondering how things had changed so fast. What could he have done to make Joe so unhappy with him that he would fire him? He puzzled over it as he walked home.

The Mystery Is Solved

Kevin ran into Tom about a week later. Tom seemed to want to turn and go the other way when he saw Kevin. Tom knew that Kevin had seen him, so he sheepishly said, "Hi, how are things going?" Kevin told him he was doing OK, but it was hard getting by without the job. He told Tom what had happened at work and how strangely Joe had acted. Tom turned red and hesitated before saying anything. Kevin wondered what was going on. Now Tom was acting weird. Tom took a deep breath and finally blurted it out: "Well, Kevin, Joe saw you with Paul. Why didn't you tell me you were gay?" Kevin didn't quite know what to say. How had his secret gotten out? "I don't know what you are taking about. Paul is my roommate." Tom said sarcastically, "Sure he is. You just go around hugging your roommate all the time?" "How did you know that?" Kevin retorted. Tom said that Joe had told him he had seen him and Paul when he had gone out the back door to receive the delivery.

Kevin told Tom this was a private matter, and he didn't want him shooting his mouth off about it. Tom told him not to worry, he wouldn't, but he didn't want to see him again. As Kevin watched Tom walk away he had a horrible feeling in the pit of his stomach. Joe must have let him go because of what he had seen that afternoon. Kevin was confused. Why hadn't Joe talked to him? Then he began to get angry. Joe had no right to fire him. He knew that he had been one of the best waiters at the Grinder. He knew that just because he was gay there was no reason to fire him. Kevin decided that something had to be done. He planned on calling his father just as soon as he got home.

◩ DISCUSSION QUESTIONS

Ethics-Related Questions

1. Based on Joe's religious values and moral beliefs, was he justified in firing Kevin?

2. Because he was aware of Joe's views about homosexuals, Kevin did not tell Joe that he was gay. If he had, Joe probably would not have hired him. Does Kevin's decision not to tell Joe that he was gay raise any moral or ethical issue that would come up if Kevin decides to take legal action against Joe for firing him? Discuss.

HRM-Related Questions

1. Legally, did Joe have a right to fire Kevin? Discuss and debate.

2. Because homosexuals are not considered a protected-class group, does Kevin have any legal recourse against Joe for firing him?

References

Ackerman, R. W., & Bauer, R. A. (1976). *Corporate social responsiveness.* Reston, VA: Reston.

Aikman, D., & Jackson, D. S. (1993, Fall). Not quite so welcome anymore. *Time, 142*(21, Special issue), 10-12.

Akers, J. (1989). Ethics and competitiveness: Putting first things first. *Sloan Management Review, 30,* 69-71.

America's welcome mat is wearing thin. (1992, July 13). *Business Week,* p. 119.

American Management Association. (1995). *AMA survey on managing cultural diversity.* New York: Author.

American Standard's executive melting pot. (1993, July 2). *Business Week,* pp. 92-93.

Anderson, C. R. (1984). *Management skills, functions, and organization performance.* Dubuque, IA: William C. Brown.

Andrew, T. (1988, May 16). Samsung: South Korea marches to its own drummer. *Forbes,* pp. 84-89.

Andrews, K. R. (1989, September-October). Ethics in practice. *Harvard Business Review,* pp. 99-104.

Arlow, R., & Ulrich, T. A. (1980). Auditing your organization's ethics. *Internal Auditor, 39*(4), 26-31.

Arogyaswamy, B., & Byles, C. (1987). Organizational culture: Internal and external fits. *Journal of Management Studies, 13*(4), 647-659.

Axtell, R. E. (1985). *Do's and taboos around the world.* New York: John Wiley.

Barney, J. B. (1986). Organizational culture: Can it be a source of sustained competitive advantage? *Academy of Management Review, 2*(3), 656-665.

Beauchamp, T. L. (1982). *Philosophical ethics: An introduction to moral philosophy.* New York: McGraw-Hill.

Beauchamp, T. L., & Bowie, N. E. (1983). *Ethical theory and business.* Englewood Cliffs, NJ: Prentice Hall.

Bennett, A. (1986, February 12). American culture is often a puzzle for foreign managers in the U.S. *Wall Street Journal*, p. 29.

Bennett, A. (1988, July 15). Ethics codes spread despite skepticism. *Wall Street Journal*, p. 19.

Best, J. R. (1992). Morality. In P. Mussen (Ed.), *Carmichael's manual of child psychology* (4th ed., Vol. 3). New York: John Wiley.

Blanchard, K., & Peale, N. V. (1988). *The power of ethical management*. New York: William Morrow.

Blonston, G. (1992, December 4). The face of America to change by 2050. *Daily Camera*, p. 4A.

Bose, P. P. (1993). An economic iron curtain? *McKinley Quarterly, 19*(1), 23-24.

Boyacigiller, N. A., & Adler, N. (1991). The parochial dinosaur: Organizational science in a global context. *Academy of Management Review, 16,* 262-290.

Buchanan, B. (1974, December). Building organizational commitment: The socialization of managers in work organizations. *Administrative Science Quarterly*, pp. 114-127.

Buchanan, B. (1975, Spring). To walk an extra mile—The whats, whens, and whys of organizational commitment. *Organizational Dynamics*, pp. 42-57.

Buchholz, R. A. (1989). *Fundamental concepts and problems in business ethics*. Englewood Cliffs, NJ: Prentice Hall.

Buchowicz, B. (1990). Cultural transition and attitude change. *Journal of General Management, 15,* 45-55.

Buller, P. F., Kohls, J. J., & Anderson, K. S. (1991). The challenge of global ethics. *Journal of Business Ethics, 10,* 767-775.

Buonocore, A. J. (1992). Managing diversity. *Management Review, 81,* 55-57.

Business Roundtable. (1988). *Corporate ethics: A prime business asset*. New York: Author.

Butler, K. (1993, November). Toward a bias-free workplace. *Training & Development*, pp. 47-49.

Byrne, J. A. (1988, February 15). Businesses are signing up for Ethics 101. *Business Week*, pp. 56-57.

Byrnes, N. (1995, July 10). Dialing for dinero. *Business Week*, p. 108.

Byron, S. J. (1977, November). The meaning of business ethics. *Business Horizons*, p. 32.

Campbell, J. P., Dunnette, M. D., Lawler, E. E., & Weick, K. E. (1970). *Managerial behavior, performance, and effectiveness*. New York: McGraw-Hill.

Chatov, R. (1980, Summer). What corporate ethics statements say. *California Management Review*, p. 22.

Cohen, J. R., Pant, L. W., & Sharp, D. J. (1992, September). Cultural and socioeconomic constraints on international codes of ethics. *Journal of Business Ethics*, pp. 687-699.

Cole, D. (1993, December 13). Texas commission relents, awards Apple tax break. *MacWeek*, p. 1.

Coleman, T. (1994, October). Managing diversity: Keeping it in focus. *Public Management*, pp. 10-16.

Coors extends workers' benefits to unmarried and gay partners. (1995, July 8). *Daily Camera*, p. D6.

Davis, K. (1957). *Human relations in business*. New York: McGraw-Hill.

Davis, K., & Newstrom, J. W. (1985). *Human behavior at work: Organizational behavior*. New York: McGraw-Hill.

Davis, S. M. (1985, July). Who are we? *Public Relations Journal,* pp. 14-44.

Deal, T. E., & Kennedy, A. A. (1982). *Corporate cultures*. Reading, MA: Addison-Wesley.

de Bettignies, H.-C. (1991, September). *Ethics and international business: A European perspective*. Paper presented at the Tokyo conference on the ethics of business in a global economy, Kashiwa-Shi, Japan.

De Cenzo, D. A. (1988). *Management*. Englewood Cliffs, NJ: Prentice Hall.

Drake, B. H., & Drake, E. (1988, Winter). Ethical and legal aspects of managing corporate culture. *California Management Review,* pp. 120-121.

Dubin, R., Champoux, J. E., & Porter, L. W. (1975, September). Central life interests and organizational commitment of blue-collar and clerical workers. *Administrative Science Quarterly,* pp. 411-421.

Dwyer, P., & Cuneo, A. Z. (1991, July 8). The "other minorities" demand their due. *Business Week,* p. 62.

Ellis, J. E. (1991, July 8). Monsanto's new challenge: Keeping minority workers. *Business Week,* pp. 60-61.

Elson, J. (1993, Fall). The great migration. *Time, 142*(21, Special issue), 28-33.

Elton, H. (1992). Still the luck country. *Australian Accountant, 62*(2), 32-35.

England, G. W. (1975). *The manager and his values*. Cambridge, MA: Ballinger.

Epstein, A. (1996, July 2). Justices reject affirmative action admissions rules. *Daily Camera,* p. 1A.

Evans, M. S. (1994). *The theme is freedom: Religion, politics and the American tradition*. Washington, DC: Regnery.

Ferrell, O. C., & Skinner, S. J. (1988). Ethical behavior and bureaucratic structure in marketing research organizations. *Journal of Marketing Research, 25,* 103-109.

Ferrell, O. C., Zey-Ferrell, M., & Krugman, D. (1983). A comparison of predictors of ethical and unethical behavior among corporate and agency advertising managers. *Journal of Macromarketing, 3*(1), 19-21.

Fisse, B., & Braithwaite, J. (1983). *The impact of publicity on corporate offenders*. Albany: State University of New York Press.

Forehand, G. A., & Gilmer, B. V. H. (1964, December). Environmental variation in studies of organizational behavior. *Psychological Bulletin,* pp. 363-382.

Frantz, D. (1988, August 15). American women, minorities complain of bias on the job. *The Tribune,* pp. B3-B5.

Frederick, W. C. (1978). *From CSR1 to CSR2: The maturing of business and society thought* (Working Paper No. 279). Pittsburgh, PA: University of Pittsburgh, Graduate School of Business.

Frederick, W. C. (1985). Toward CSR3: The normative factor in corporate social analysis. In *Proceedings of the Academy of Management Forty-Fifth Annual Meeting* (pp. 16-17). San Diego: Academy of Management.

Frederick, W. C., Davis, K., & Post, J. E. (1988). *Business and society: Corporate strategy, public policy, and ethics*. New York: McGraw-Hill.

Freeman, R. E., & Gilbert, D. R., Jr. (1988). *Corporate strategy and the search for ethics.* Englewood Cliffs, NJ: Prentice Hall.

Friedman, M. (1970, September 13). The social responsibility of business is to increase its profits. *New York Times Magazine,* pp. 122-126.

Fritzsche, D. J., & Becker, H. (1984). Linking management behavior to ethical philosophy: An empirical investigation. *Academy of Management Journal, 9,* 166-175.

Fry, J. N., & Killing, J. P. (1986). *Strategic analysis and action.* Englewood Cliffs, NJ: Prentice Hall.

Galen, M., & Palmer, A. T. (1994, January 31). White, male, and worried. *Business Week,* pp. 50-55.

Garvin, D. (1993). Building a learning organization. *Harvard Business Review, 71,* 78-91.

Gerloff, E. A. (1985). *Organizational theory and design: A strategic approach for management.* New York: McGraw-Hill.

Getter, L., & Alvarez, L. (1994, January 9). Lost in America: Our failed immigration policy. *Sunday Camera,* p. E1.

Gifford, N. (1983). *When in Rome: An introduction to relativism and knowledge.* Albany: State University of New York Press.

Gleckman, H., Smart, T., Dwyer, P., Segal, T., & Weber, J. (1991, July 8). Race in the workplace: Is affirmative action working? *Business Week,* pp. 50-62.

Goffman, E. (1981). *Forms of talk.* Philadelphia: University of Pennsylvania Press.

Gomez, J. E. A. (1993). Mexican corporate culture. *Business Mexico, 3*(8), 8-9.

Goodman, N. (1990a). *Doing business in Japan.* Randolph, NJ: Global Dynamics.

Goodman, N. (1990b). *Doing business overseas.* Randolph, NJ: Global Dynamics.

Gordon, J. (1992, January). Rethinking diversity. *Training Magazine,* pp. 1-9.

Gregory, K. (1983). Native-view paradigms: Multiple cultures and culture conflicts in organizations. *Administrative Science Quarterly, 28,* 450-467.

Gutierrez, S. (1993, March-April). Can you make it in Mexico? *Financial Executive,* pp. 20-23.

Hall, E. T. (1981). *Beyond culture.* New York: Doubleday.

Harrington, S. J. (1991). What corporate America is teaching about ethics. *Academy of Management Executive, 5*(1), 21-30.

Harris executive poll. (1991, July 8). *Business Week,* p. 63.

Hegarty, W. H., & Sims, H. P. (1979). Organizational philosophy, policies, and objectives related to unethical decision behavior: A laboratory experiment. *Journal of Applied Psychology, 64*(3), 331-338.

Hertz, D. L. (1991). Developing management skills in Eastern Europe. *Journal of European Business, 3*(1), 60-61.

Higgins, J. M. (1991). *The management challenge.* New York: Macmillan.

Higgins, J. M., & Vincze, J. W. (1993). *Strategic management concepts.* Fort Worth, TX: Dryden.

Hodgson, K. (1992). Adapting ethical decisions to a global marketplace. *Management Review, 8*(15), 53-57.

Hoffman, W. M. (1989). Business ethics in the United States: Its past decade and its future. *Business Insights, 5,* 6-13.

Hofstede, G. (1980). *Culture's consequences: International differences in work-related values.* Beverly Hills, CA: Sage.

Hofstede, G. (1984). *Culture's consequences: International differences in work-related values* (abridged edition). Beverly Hills, CA: Sage.

Hofstede, G., Nevijen, B., & Sanders, G. (1990). Measuring organizational cultures: A qualitative and quantitative study across twenty cases. *Administrative Science Quarterly, 35,* 375-392.

Holmquist, D. (1993). Ethics: How important is it in today's office? *Public Personnel Management, 22,* 537-544.

Hopkins, W. E., & Hopkins, S. A. (1990). The strategic management of cultural risk in domestic firms. *International Journal of Management, 7,* 158-165.

Ivancevich, J. M., Szilagyi, A. D., Jr., & Wallace, M. J., Jr. (1977). *Organizational behavior and performance.* Santa Monica, CA: Goodyear Publishing.

Jain, H. C. (1991). Is there a coherent human resource management system in India? *International Journal of Manpower, 12*(1), 10-17.

Jamieson, E. L., & Seaman, B. (1993, Fall). America's immigrant challenge. *Time, 142*(21, Special issue), 3-9.

Jamieson, D., & O'Mara, J. (1991). *Managing workforce 2000: Gaining the diversity advantage.* San Francisco: Jossey-Bass.

Jamieson, D., & O'Mara, J. (1992, February). Managing workforce 2000. *Small Business Reports,* pp. 68-71.

Johnson, B. (1993, January 18). The gay quandary. *Advertising Age,* pp. 29-35.

Johnston, W. B., & Packer, A. (1987). *Workforce 2000: Work and workers for the 21st century.* Indianapolis, IN: Hudson Institute.

Jones, G. R. (1986). Socialization tactics, self-efficacy, and newcomers' adjustments to organizations. *Academy of Management Journal, 29,* 262-279.

Kalish, D. E. (1995, February 10). Ex-AT&T official in insider trading scam. *Daily Camera,* p. A14.

Kant, I. (1964). *Groundwork of the metaphysics of morals.* New York: Harper & Row.

Karp, H. B., & Abramms, B. (1992, August). Doing the right thing. *Training & Development,* pp. 37-41.

Kasper, W. (1992). Advancing into the 21st century: Visions and challenges facing the downunder economy. *Australian Economic Review, 100,* 51-54.

Keefe, S. E. (1992). Ethnic identity: The domain of perceptions of and attachment to ethnic groups and cultures. *Human Organizations, 51*(1), 35-43.

Kidder, R. M. (1992, March-April). Ethics: A matter of survival. *Futurist,* p. 12.

Kidron, A. (1978, June). Work values and organizational commitment. *Academy of Management Journal,* pp. 239-247.

Kramer, H. E. (1993). Doing business in Germany and Australia: An etic-emic study of contrasts. *Management Decision, 30*(4), 52-56.

Lacayo, R. (1993, Fall). The "cultural" defense. *Time, 142*(21, Special issue), 61.

Laurent, A. (1983). The cultural diversity of Western conceptions of management. *International Studies of Management and Organization, 13,* 75-96.

Lee, D., & Tefft, S. (1989, May 1). India is becoming the new Asian magnet for U.S. business. *Business Week*, p. 132.

Likert, R. (1967). *The human organization*. New York: McGraw-Hill.

Madsen, P. (1991, Fall). Responsible design and the management of ethics. *Design Management Journal*, pp. 9-12.

Madsen, P., & Shafritz, J. M. (1990). *Essentials of business ethics*. New York: Meridian.

Malic, M., Rees, J., Johnstone, B., Chang, F., & Knowles, R. (1992). Australia 1992: Paul primes the pump. *Far Eastern Economic Review, 155*(14), 33-45.

Mandell, B., & Kohler-Gray, S. (1990, March). Management development that values diversity. *Personnel*, pp. 41-47.

Manor, R. (1991, July 18). Brewers aim intoxicating malt liquor at blacks. *Rocky Mountain News*, pp. 54-55.

March, J. G., & Simon, H. A. (1958). *Organizations*. New York: John Wiley.

Martin, J., & Siehl, C. (1983). Organizational culture and counter culture: An uneasy symbiosis. *Organizational Dynamics, 12*(2), 52-64.

McCoy, C. (1975). *Ethics in the corporate policy process: An introduction*. Berkeley, CA: Center for Ethics and Social Policy, Graduate Theological Union.

McCoy, C. S. (1985). *Management of values: The ethical difference in corporate policy and performance*. Boston: Pitman.

McCuddy, M. K., Reichardt, K. E., & Schroeder, D. L. (1993, April). Ethical pressures: Fact or fiction? *Management Accounting*, pp. 57-61.

McHugh, F. P. (1988). *Keyguide to information sources in business ethics*. New York: Nichols.

McLaughlin, R. (1990). *Marketing in the United Kingdom* (Overseas Business Reports, No. 5). Washington, DC: U.S. Department of Commerce, International Trade Administration.

McMenamin, B. (1995, May 22). Diversity hucksters. *Forbes*, pp. 174-176.

Miller, K. C. (1992, July 20). Mainstream marketers decide time is right to target gays. *Marketing News*, pp. 8-15.

Mills, D. Q., & Cannon, M. D. (1989, August). Managing baby boomers. *Management Review*, pp. 38-42.

Mitchell, R., & O'Neal, M. (1994, August 1). Managing by values. *Business Week*, pp. 46-52.

Munter, M. (1993, May-June). Cross-cultural communication for managers. *Business Horizons*, pp. 69-77.

Murphy, P. E. (1988). Implementing business ethics. *Journal of Business Ethics, 7,* 907-915.

Nemetz, P. L., & Christensen, S. L. (1996). The challenge of cultural diversity: Harnessing a diversity of views to understand multiculturalism. *Academy of Management Review, 21,* 434-462.

Nicholls, R. F. (1992). The neglected service industries of Eastern Europe: Some quantitative and qualitative aspects. *International Journal of Service Industry Management, 3*(3), 46-61.

Ohmae, K. (1989). *The borderless world: Power and strategy in the interlinked economy.* New York: Harper.

O'Reilly, C. (1989). Corporations, culture and commitment: Motivation and social control in organizations. *California Management Review, 31*(4), 9-25.

Orr, J. (1993). Back in Tokyo. *CAE, 12*(3), 56.

Payne, R. L., & Pugh, D. S. (1976). Organization structure and climate. In M. D. Dunnette (Ed.), *Handbook of organizational and industrial psychology* (pp. 1125-1173). Chicago: Rand McNally.

Pascale, R. T. (1985). The paradox of culture: Reconciling ourselves to socialization. *California Management Review, 27,* 26-41.

Pearce, J. A., & Robinson, R. B. (1994). *Formulation, implementation, and control of competitive strategy.* Homewood, IL: Irwin.

Permutter, H. V., & Heenan, D. A. (1984). How multinational should your top managers be? *Harvard Business Review, 53,* 121-132.

Pettit, J. D., Jr., Vaught, B., & Pulley, K. J. (1990). The role of communication in organizations: Ethical considerations. *Journal of Business Communication, 27*(3), 233-249.

Petty, R. E., & Cacioppo, J. T. (1990). *Attitudes and persuasion: Classic and contemporary approaches.* Dubuque, IA: William C. Brown.

Piturro, M., & Mahoney, S. S. (1991, May-June). Managing diversity: The new multicultural workforce requires a simpatico style. *Executive Female,* pp. 45-48.

Posner, B. Z., & Schmidt, W. H. (1994, Spring). Values and the American manager: An update updated. *California Management Review,* pp. 80-93.

Primeaux, P. (1992). Experiential ethics: A blueprint for personal and corporate ethics. *Journal of Business Ethics, 11*(10), 779-787.

Radebaugh, D. O. (1976). *International business: Environments and operations.* Reading, MA: Addison-Wesley.

Randall, D. M. (1987). Commitment and the organization: The organization man revisited. *Academy of Management Review, 12*(3), 460-471.

Ratio, I., & Rodgers, I. (1984). A workshop on cultural differences. *AFS Orientation Handbook,* p. 4.

Rawls, J. (1971). *A theory of justice.* Cambridge, MA: Belknap.

Reynolds, L. (1992, October). America's work ethic: Lost in turbulent times? *Management Review,* pp. 20-25.

Robin, D. P., & Reidenbach, R. E. (1987). Social responsibility, ethics, and marketing strategy: Closing the gap between concept and application. *Journal of Marketing, 51,* 44-58.

Robin, D. P., & Reidenbach, R. E. (1989). *Business ethics: Where profits meet value systems.* Englewood Cliffs, NJ: Prentice Hall.

Rokeach, M. (1968). *Beliefs, attitudes, and values.* San Francisco: Jossey-Bass.

Schauffler, R. (1994). Children of immigrants. *National Forum, 74,* 37-40.

Schein, E. (1983, Summer). The role of the founder in creating organizational culture. *Organizational Dynamics,* pp. 13-28.

Schuler, R. S., Galiente, S. P., & Jackson, S. E. (1987, September). Matching effective human resource practices with competitive strategy. *Personnel,* pp. 18-27.

Schwartz, H., & Davis, S. M. (1981, Summer). Matching corporate culture and business strategy. *Organizational Dynamics,* pp. 30-48.

Sen, S. (1993). Japan. In *International business interact* [computer database]. Mountain Lakes, NJ: ABI.

Sen, S. (1993). United Kingdom (Britain). In *International business interact* [computer database]. Mountain Lakes, NJ: ABI.

Sheedy, J. (1990, September-October). The work force of tomorrow. *Harvard Business Review,* pp. 234-235.

Shimko, B. W. (1992, May-June). Pre-hire assessment of the new work force: Finding wheat (and work ethic) among the chaff. *Business Horizons,* pp. 60-65.

Sims, R. R. (1992). The challenge of ethical behavior in organizations. *Journal of Business Ethics, 11,* 505-513.

Sinclair, A. (1993). Approaches to organizational culture and ethics. *Journal of Business Ethics, 12,* 63-73.

Singer, A. W. (1992, March). The ultimate ethics test. *Across the Board,* pp. 18-22.

Singh, A. (1993). Growth of urban centres, trade, commerce and industry in the Delhi sultanate. *Employment News, 18*(22), 1-2.

Singh, J. P., & Hofstede, G. (1990). Managerial culture and work-related values in India: Reply and comment. *Organization Studies, 11*(1), 75-106.

Sinha, B. M. (1992). India: Towards a social revolution. *Futures, 24*(9), 895-906.

Solomon, C. M. (1991, November). Are white males being left out? *Personnel Journal,* pp. 88-94.

Soloman, C. M. (1993, February). Managing today's immigrants. *Personnel Journal,* pp. 57-65.

Steers, R. M. (1977). *Organizational effectiveness: A behavioral view.* Santa Monica, CA: Goodyear Publishing.

Steiner, G. A., & Miner, J. B. (1977). *Management policy and strategy: Text, readings, and cases.* New York: Macmillan.

Steward, S., Cheung, M. T., & Yeung, D. W. K. (1992). The South China economic community: The latest Asian newly industrialized economy emerges. *Columbia Journal of World Business, 27*(2), 30-37.

Stewart, J. (1991, December 16). Gay in corporate America. *Fortune,* pp. 42-56.

Stoner, J. A., & Freeman, R. E. (1989). *Management.* Englewood Cliffs, NJ: Prentice Hall.

Swartz, J. (1993, December 6). Apple may scrap plans to expand near Austin: Anti-gay vote blocks $750,000 tax break. *MacWeek,* p. 24.

Thiederman, S. (1991). *Bridging cultural barriers for corporate success: How to manage the multicultural work force.* Los Angeles: Lexington Books.

Toobin, J. (1996, July 8). Supreme sacrifice. *New Yorker,* pp. 43-47.

Touche-Ross Foundation. (1988). *Ethics in American business: An opinion survey of key business leaders on ethical standards and behavior.* Detroit: Author.

Tung, R. C. (1993). Managing cross-national and intranational diversity. *Human Resource Management, 32*(4), 461-477.

Tunstall, W. B. (1983). Cultural transition at AT&T. *Sloan Management Review, 2,* 15-26.

U.S. Bureau of the Census. (1992). *Statistical abstract of the United States* (112th ed.). Washington, DC: Government Printing Office.

U.S. Bureau of Labor Statistics. (1991). *Statistical abstract of the United States* (111th ed.). Washington, DC: Government Printing Office.

Velasquez, M. (1983, Spring). Why corporations are not morally responsible for anything they do. *Business and Professional Ethics Journal*, pp. 1-18.

Velasquez, M. G. (1982). *Business ethics: Concepts and cases.* Englewood Cliffs, NJ: Prentice Hall.

Vitell, S., & Festervand, T. (1987). Business ethics: Conflict, practices and beliefs of industrial executives. *Journal of Business Ethics, 6,* 111-122.

Vitell, S. J., Nwachukwu, S. L., & Barnes, J. H. (1993). The effects of culture on ethical decision making: An application of Hofstede's typology. *Journal of Business Ethics, 12,* 753-760.

Vogel, D. (1992, Fall). The globalization of business ethics: Why America remains distinctive. *California Management Review*, pp. 30-49.

Werhane, P. H. (1985). *Persons, rights, corporations.* Englewood Cliffs, NJ: Prentice Hall.

Where the new wave of immigrants are going. (1991, September 9). *Fortune*, p. 14.

Wilkins, A., & Ouchi, W. (1983). Efficient cultures: Exploring the relationship between culture and organizational performance. *Administrative Science Quarterly, 28,* 468-481.

Williams, J. C., DuBrin, A. J., & Sisk, H. L. (1985). *Management and organization.* Cincinnati, OH: South-Western Publishing.

Wines, W. A., & Napier, N. K. (1989, March). *Toward an understanding of cross-cultural ethics: A model.* Paper presented at the annual meeting of the Western Academy of Management, San Francisco.

Wisdom, J. (1970). *Tolerance in paradox and discovery.* Berkeley: University of California Press.

Wolin, S. S. (1993). Democracy, difference, and re-cognition. *Political Theory, 21,* 464-484.

Wood, D. J. (1990). *Business and society.* Glenview, IL: Scott, Foresman.

Wright, P., Ferris, S. P., Hiller, J. S., & Kroll, M. (1995). Competitiveness through management of diversity: Effects on stock price valuation. *Academy of Management Journal, 38,* 272-287.

Zeiger, D. (1992, October 27). Women will dominate the 21st century workforce. *Business Plus*, pp. 6-7.

Zinn, L., Power, C., Yang, D. J., Cuneo, A. Z., & Ross, D. (1992, December 14). Move over, boomers. *Business Week*, pp. 74-82.

Index

Abramms, B., 16, 25, 103
Accommodating:
    disabled employees, 152
    religious differences, 135-136
Accommodation:
    Asian cultural value of, 38
    carriers of nonmainstream ethical values, 94
Achievement, American value system and, 44
Achievement motivation, 81
Ackerman, R. W., 109
Actions:
    consequences of, 26, 31
    ethical standards for, 25
    evaluating, 24
    individual responsibility for, 27-28
    moral, 25-26
    translating strategy into, 74-75
Adler, N., 19
Affirmative action, 101, 114
African Americans:
    baby busters, 13
    in management, 85
    values of, 45-46
    workforce participation, 12
Age, 3
    East Indian culture and, 40
    issues about, 153-154
Age Discrimination in Employment Act, 90
Age diversity, defined, 5
Age groups, 13

Aikman, D., 4, 9, 10
Akers, J., 57
Alvarez, L., 18
Ambiguity, tolerance of, 48-49
America:
    ethical/moral character of, 4-5, 8
    foreign-owned companies in, 88-89
    moral code in, 30
    moral traditions in, 15
    salient features of society, 4
    subcultures, 44-46
    value system, 44-45
American culture:
    dimensions of, 47
    mainstream values, 15
    time orientation and, 37
American managers, ethical behavior of, 92
American Standard Inc., 89
Americans with Disabilities Act, 90
Anderson, C. R., 92
Anderson, K. S., 25, 59, 61, 94
Andrews, K. R., 77
Anglican religion, 42
Apple Computer Company, 7
Arab managers, hiring women and, 88
Arlow, R., 104
Arogyaswamy, B., 35
Asia, immigration from, 10
Asian Americans:
    baby busters, 13
    cultural values, 45

deculturation and, 45
  white-collar jobs, 86
  workforce participation, 12
Asian cultures, 38-40
  dimensions of, 47
  employees from, 113
Asian managers, hiring women and, 88
Asian organizations, corporate culture in, 38
Assimilation, 45, 58-59, 61
Asylum seekers, 10
AT&T, 57-58, 109
Attitudes:
  geocentric, 88
  underlying, 24
  work, 79-81
Australian managers, ethical behavior of, 92
Australian value system, 43-44
Authority:
  Asian cultures, 38
  Australian value system and, 43
  individual, 36
  Latin culture and, 41
  religious, 36

Baby boomers, 5, 13
Baby busters, 5, 13
Balkin, D. B., 148-150
Barnes, J. H., 49
Barney, J. B., 75
Bauer, R. A., 109
Beauchamp, T. L., 5, 29
Becker, H., 31
Behavior:
  codes of ethics focusing on, 103
  responsibility for, 15
  See also Ethical behavior
Beliefs:
  corporate culture, 57
  underlying, 24
Bennett, A., 60
Best, J. R., 26
Bible, Western society and, 36
Bisexuality, 3, 5
Blanchard, K., 111
Blonston, G., 12
Boards of directors, composition of, 110
Boorstin, D., 8
Bowie, N. E., 5

Boyacigiller, N. A., 19
Braithwaite, J., 57
Bribes, 41, 60
Britain, 42, 43
Buchanan, B., 75
Buchholz, R. A., 17, 105
Buchowicz, B., 58
Buddhism, 38, 40
Buller, P. F., 25, 59, 61, 94
Bumpus, M. A., 148-150
Buonocore, A. J., 69
Business ethics, diversity implications for,
  105-115
Business Roundtable, 72, 82
Butler, K., 86, 87
Byles, C., 35
Byrnes, N., 109, 110
Byron, S. J., 24, 25

Cacioppo, J. T., 58
California, Proposition 187 and, 114
Campbell, J. P., 99
Cannon, M. D., 13
Caribbean, immigration from, 10
Caring, in Japanese culture, 39
Cases, 117-160
Caste system, 40
Central America, immigration from, 10
Champoux, J. E., 80
Chatov, R., 60
Checklists, defining ethics in terms of, 27
Chinese values, 122-124
Christensen, S. L., 27
Christianity, 36
  East Indian culture and, 40
  Western European value system and, 42
Civil Rights Act of 1964, 90
Class, *see* Social position
Cleanliness, American value system and,
  44
Codes of conduct, 59-61
Codes of ethics, *see* Ethical codes
Cognate industries, 109
Cohen, J. R., 15-16
Cole, D., 7
Coleman, T., 111-112
Collective conscience, 36
Collectivist cultures, 46, 47, 49-50

clusters of, 53
social group relativism and, 29
unethical conduct and, 97
Color, 5
Colorado, anti-gay-rights amendment in, 7
Communicating values, corporate culture
    and, 17
Communication:
    cultural network and, 18
    diversity and, 16
    problems in, 68-69
Community, corporation as, 17
Community support for organization, 78
Competitiveness:
    American value system and, 44
    organizational, 72-73, 74
Concepts, ethics-related, 23-33
Conduct, codes of, 59-61
Confidentiality, 60
Conflict(s):
    ethical, 81
    racial-related, 148-149
Conflicting values, 68-69
Conflicts of interest, 60
Conformity:
    Japanese culture and, 39
    pressure and, 59
Confucianism, 38, 39
Consensus, subcultures and, 35
Control, internal versus external, 37
Coors Brewing Company, 7
Core values, 19
    corporate culture and, 57
Corporate America, 6
Corporate codes of ethics, 14-15, 60, 102-103
Corporate culture:
    Asian organizations, 38
    coalitions of subcultures and, 34
    core values and, 19
    cultural dimensions and, 98-99
    cultural networks and, 16
    defining, 17-18, 57
    destabilization of, 63-70
    effectiveness of, 58-59
    employee commitment and, 73-74
    employee selection and, 95-102
    ethics and, 57-59
    ethics and organizational performance
        and, 73-74

influences on, 56
Japanese organizations, 39
learning, 101
profile, 100-101
regulating ethics through, 57-58
strategy implementation and, 75
unethical behavior and, 76-77
Corporate culture foreigners, 87
Corporate culture natives, 86-87
Countries:
    cultural clusters, 52
    cultural dimensions, 47
Courtesy:
    Asian cultures and, 38
    Japanese culture and, 39
Cross-cultural perspectives, on managerial
    ethics, 88-90
Cultural clusters, 37-46, 51-53
    HRM framework, 99
Cultural differences, 35, 45
Cultural dimensions, 37-46
    corporate culture and, 98-99
    ethical values and, 46-53
    unethical behavior and, 97-98
    work ethic and, 81
Cultural diversity:
    defined, 5
    ethical diversity and, 15-16
    ethics and, 4-6
Cultural network, 65
    core values and, 19
    corporate culture and, 16
    defined, 18
Cultural relativism, 5-6, 29-30
Cultural themes, 37
Cultural values, organizational ethics and,
    55-56
Cultural value systems, 37-46
Cuneo, A. Z., 13, 86
Customs, 30, 57

Davis, K., 17, 18, 76, 80, 99
Davis, S. M., 75
Deal, T. E., 77
De Bettignies, H.-C., 60
De Cenzo, D. A., 37
Deculturation, 45
Demeanor, Japanese culture and, 39

Democratic principles, British value system and, 43
Demographic(s), 8-14
Demographic descriptors, 3
Deontological norms:
    cultural clusters and, 52-53
    uncertainty avoidance cultures and, 49
Deontological perspective:
    managerial values and, 92
    religion and, 36
Deontological theories of ethics, 26
Descriptive ethics, 16-17, 24
Descriptors, types of, 3
Differential association theory, 48
Disability diversity, defined, 5
Disabled employees, 151-155
Discrimination, 32
    against homosexuals, 14, 19, 156-160
    in Australia, 44
    foreign-owned companies and, 89
    in hiring, 102
    laws and, 89, 90
    lawsuits and, 21
    reverse, 120
Distributive justice, 31, 83
Diverse cultures, ethical values in, 34-54
Diverse ethical values, reconciling, 94-104
Diversity:
    business social responsibility to, 107-108
    business social responsiveness to, 108-110
    current level of, 63-70
    ethical codes and, 61
    ethical concepts and, 23-33
    ethical values and, 55-71
    ethics paradigms and, 14-22
    implications for business ethics, 105-115
    managerial ethics and, 83-93
    moral obligations toward, 21-22
    moral relativism and, 27-30
    new rhetoric of, 3-4
    performance issues and, 72-81
    presuppositions about, 20-21
    realities of, 8-14
    See also Cultural diversity; Ethical diversity
Diversity training, 19
Divorce, children of, 13
Downsizing, 119-121
Drake, B. H., 103
Drake, E., 103

Dual-career households, children of, 13
Dubin, R., 80
DuBrin, A. J., 91
Dunnette, M. D., 99
Duties, ethical standards based on, 26, 27
Dwyer, P., 85, 86

Eastern cultures, *see* Asian cultures
Eastern European cultures, 41-42
    dimensions of, 47
East Indian culture, 39-40
    dimensions of, 47
    managerial behavior, 92Economic background, 3
Economic goals, 74
Economic values, 91
Education, 3
    East Indian culture and, 40
    Latin culture and, 40
    Western European value system and, 43
Egalitarianism, Western European organizations and, 43
Ellis, J. E., 85
Elson, J., 8
Emotions:
    British value system and, 43
    Eastern European value system and, 41
Employee commitment:
    corporate culture and, 73-74
    role of ethical/unethical behavior and, 76-77
    strategy implementation and, 75-76
Employees:
    hiring, 95-102
    rights of, 83
Enforcing values, corporate culture and, 17
England, G. W., 91
England, *see* Britain
English as a second language, 18-19
Enlightened self-interest, 91
Epstein, A., 114
Equal opportunity, 89-90, 101-102
Equity, 83
Ethic(s):
    corporate culture and, 57-59
    cultural diversity and, 4-6
    defining, 5, 21, 24
    human diversity and, 6-7

human resources management and, 95-102
interrelationship among factors, 55-56
morality and, 25-26
performance issues and, 72-81
realities of diversity and, 8-14
training in, 60-61, 103
values and, 24-25
See also Descriptive ethics; Normative
    ethics;
Prescriptive ethics
Ethical behavior:
    employee commitment effects, 76
    learning from peers, 48, 97
    responsibility for, 15
Ethical codes, 14-15, 102
    applying, 25
    diversity and, 61
    in organizations, 59-61
Ethical concepts, 23-33
Ethical conflicts, 81
Ethical diversity, cultural diversity and, 15-16
Ethical frameworks, origins of, 32-33
Ethical/moral approach to managerial values,
    92
Ethical power for organizations, 111
Ethical standards, 4
Ethical synergy, human resources
    management and, 96-102
Ethical values:
    cultural dimensions and, 46-53
    diversity and, 55-71
    in diverse cultures, 34-54
    influences on, 56
    reconciling diverse, 94-104
    religion and, 36-37
Ethical violations, 83
Ethics-diversity process model, 16-20, 63
Ethics paradigms, 14-22
    cultural dimensions and, 51
    defining, 16-17
    interrelated, 55-56
    nature of, 61-71
    performance and, 77-80
    shifts in, 5, 6, 28-30, 55-57, 63-71, 78, 94
    violation of, 28-29
Ethics-related theories, 113
Ethnic culture, American subcultures and, 45
Ethnic differences, 35
Ethnic identities:

perpetuating, 3
reactive, 59
Ethnic minorities, 12-13. *See also* Minorities
Ethnographic descriptors, 3
Ethos, 24
Europe:
    Eastern, 41-42, 47
    immigration from, 10
    Western, 42-43, 47
European American values, 45
Evans, M. S., 36

Facial expressions, communicating through,
    19
Fairness, 83
Fair play:
    American value system and, 44
    Australian value system and, 44
    British value system and, 43
Family:
    Chinese values and, 122-123
    French value system and, 43
    Latin culture and, 40, 129-130
Family unification, immigration law
    stressing, 9
Family values right, 14
Feelings, *see* Emotions
Feelings of others, Asian cultures and, 38
Feminine cultures, 46, 47, 50
    achievement motivation and, 81
    clusters of, 53
    unethical conduct and, 98
Ferrell, O, C., 48, 49, 97
Ferris, S. P., 77
Festervand, T., 104
Fisse, B., 57
Forehand, G. A., 99
Foreign-owned companies, in United States,
    88-89
Formality:
    Asian cultures and, 38
    Australian value system and, 44
    Japanese culture and, 39
    Latin culture and, 41
    Western European organizations and, 43
France, 42, 43
Frantz, D., 88, 89
Frederick, W. C., 18, 32, 108

Free expression, right to, 32
Freeman, R. E., 28, 61
Friedman, M., 21
Fritzsche, D. J., 31
Fry, J. N., 74
Future orientation, 37

Galen, M., 87
Galiente, S. P., 95
Garvin, D., 65
Gay rights, 7
Gender, 3
Gender diversity, defined, 5
General Electric Corporation, 60, 65
Generalized corporate culture profile, 100-101
General Motors, 21
Generation X, *see* Baby busters
Geocentric attitudes, 88
Geographic diversity, defined, 5
Geography, 3, 5
Gerloff, E. A., 18
Getter, L., 18
G. Heileman Brewing Company, 108-109, 110
Gifford, N., 27, 28
Gilbert, D. R., Jr., 28
Gilmer, B. V. H., 99
Gleckman, H., 85, 86
Goffman, E., 28
Gordon, J., 21
Government intervention, 108-109, 110
Great Britain, *see* Britain
Gregory, K., 35
Group, morality relative to, 29
Group ethics, influences on, 56
Group identification:
    Asian cultures, 38
    Japanese culture, 39
    See also Collectivist cultures
Guidelines, defining ethics in terms of, 27

Hall, E. T., 19
Harrington, S. J., 102
Head nodding, Eastern European value
    system and, 42
Heenan, D. A., 88
Hegarty, W. H., 50, 97
Heterosexual, 3, 5

Hewlett-Packard, 67
Hierarchies:
    Asian organizations and, 38
    Japanese culture and, 39
Higgins, J. M., 74, 95
High-context cultures, communication in,
    18-19
Hiller, J. S., 77
Hinduism, 39
Hiring:
    discrimination in, 102
    human resources management and, 95-102
    minorities, 83, 84, 85, 120, 143-145
    regulating ethical behavior and, 101-102
    white males, 86-87, 142-143
    women, 84, 88, 120, 143-145
Hispanic Americans:
    baby busters, 13
    culture, 45
    workforce participation, 12
Hispanics, in white-collar jobs, 85-86
Hodgson, K., 35, 103
Hoffman, W. M., 59
Hofstede, G., 34, 46, 51, 81, 97, 99
Holmquist, D., 60, 104
Homosexuals, 3, 5
    benefits for partners of, 7
    cultural networks, 19
    current controversies, 6-7
    discrimination against, 14, 19, 156-160
    number of, 14
Honda, 89
Hopkins, S. A., 19, 101, 119-121, 128-147,
    151-160
Hopkins, W. E., 19, 101, 125-127
Hopwood v. Texas, 114
Human diversity, ethics and, 6-7
Human resources management, 95-102
Humility, in Asian cultures, 38

Identification with organizationÆs
    objectives, 75
Immigrants, 8-11
    assimilation process, 58-59
    ethical paradigm shift and, 5
Immigration:
    illegal, 10
    legal, 9

policy, 10
U.S. attitudes toward, 114
Immigration Act of 1990, 10
Individual(s):
  American value system and, 44
  deresponsibilizing, 60
  personal code of conduct, 61
  responsible for actions, 27-28
  Western European value system and, 42
Individual authority, 36
Individual ethics, influences on, 56
Individualist cultures, 46, 47, 49-50
  clusters of, 53
  unethical conduct and, 97
Individual performance, 80-81
Individual relativism, 27-28
Individual rights, 31
Individual values, codes of ethics supporting, 103
Infiltration, 94
Insider trading, 58
Institutional support for organization, 78
Interdependence, in Japanese culture, 39
Interest group intervention, 110
Interfaith Center on Corporate Responsibility, 110
Internal control, 37
Internalization of organizational values, 75
Interpretation, 26
Involvement in work, 75
Islamic culture:
  accumulation of wealth and, 36
  East Indians and, 40
  time orientation and, 37
  work conflicts, 132-137
Ivancevich, J. M., 74

Jackson, D. S., 4, 9, 10
Jackson, S. E., 95
Jainism, 40
Jamieson, D., 13, 14, 15
Japan, women managers in, 89
Japanese managers:
  in United States, 88-89
  value orientation of, 92
Japanese organization, corporate culture in, 39
Japanese value system, 39

Jobs, equal right to, 32
Johnson & Johnson, 62-63
Johnson, B., 14
Johnston, W. B., 12
Jones, G. R., 95, 97
Judaism:
  accumulation of wealth and, 36
  East Indian culture and, 40
Justice:
  distributive, 31, 83
  foreign-owned companies and, 88-89
  procedural, 31
  promotions and, 87

Kant, I., 26
Karp, H. B., 16, 25, 103
Kennedy, A. A., 77
Kickbacks, 60
Kidder, R. M., 62
Kidron, A., 80
Killing, J. P., 74
K Mart, 21
Kohler-Gray, S., 87
Kohls, J. J., 25, 59, 61, 94
Korean managers, value orientation of, 92
Kroll, M., 77
Krugman, D., 48, 97

Lacayo, R., 6
Language, 3
Language differences, 18-19
Language diversity, defined, 5
Language skills, building, 101
Latchkey children, 13
Latin America, immigration from, 10
Latin American cultures, 40-41, 129-130
  dimensions of, 47
Latino American cultures, 45
Laurent, A., 59, 96, 101
Lawler, E. E., 99
Laws:
  antidiscrimination, 89, 90
  ethical standards based on, 26, 27
  hiring and, 102
Lawsuits, discrimination, 21
Leadership, effect on ethical behavior of, 104
Learning corporate culture, 101

Lesbians, 5
Levi Strauss & Company, 84-85
Likert, R., 99
Lockheed Corporation, 14
Low-context cultures, communication in,
18-19
Loyalty:
in Asian cultures, 38
in Japanese culture, 39
in Latin culture, 41
to organization, 75
Lucas, W. J., 148-150

Macro moral mazes, 106, 107
Macro solutions to moral mazes, 110-111
Madsen, P., 95, 102, 104, 105, 106
Majority, interests of, 31
Management committees, homosexuals on, 7
Manager(s):
accommodating diversity, 12-13
creating ethical climate, 81
Eastern European value system and, 42
East Indian culture and, 40
effectiveness of, 92-93
future challenges for, 113-114
homosexuals as, 14
Japanese organizations, 39
Latin organizations, 41
minorities as, 84, 85-86
power distance and, 48
stereotype of, 86-87
values of, 90-92
Western European organizations and, 43
Managerial ethics, diversity and, 83-93
Mandell, B., 87
Manor, R., 108
March, J. G., 75
Marriage, Latin culture and, 40
Martin, J., 34
Martin, Lynn, 89
Masculine cultures, 46, 47, 50
achievement motivation and, 81
clusters of, 53
unethical conduct and, 98
McCoy, C., 17, 24
McCuddy, M. K., 61
McHugh, F. P., 36
MCI Communications Corporation, 109

McMenamin, B., 110
Melting pot, 44
Mexico, immigration from, 10
Micro moral mazes, 106
Micro solutions to moral mazes, 111-112
Miller, K. C., 14
Mills, D. Q., 13
Miner, J. B., 76
Minorities:
on boards of directors, 110
hiring, 83, 84, 85, 120, 143-145
promoting, 83, 84, 85-86
retaining, 85
See also Ethnic minorities
Misappropriation of assets, 60
Mischief, 105-106
Mission statement, 111
Mitchell, R., 84-85
Mitsubishi Motor Manufacturing of America,
89
Modesty, in Asian cultures, 38
Money, Australian value system and, 44
Monsanto Company, 85
Moral(s), 4
Moral imperialism, 30
Morality, ethics and, 25-26
Moral mazes, 106, 107
Moral norms, 24
Moral obligations toward diversity, 21-22
Moral relativism, 27-30
Moral rights, 83
Moral standards, 25
Mos, 25
Multinational ethics, 30
Munter, M., 37
Murphy, P. E., 60

Napier, N. K., 61
Nationality, 3, 5
Native Americans:
values, 45
workforce participation, 12
Negative publicity, overshadowing moral
ambiguities, 7
Nemetz, P. L., 27
Nepotism, in Latin culture, 41
Neuborne, E., 89
Nevijen, B., 34

Newstrom, J. W., 76, 80
Nie, W., 122-124
Norm(s), 24
  accepted practice, 29
  core, 19
  corporate culture, 57
Normative ethics, 24, 112-113
Northwest Airlines, 21
Nwachukwu, S. L., 49

O'Connor, Sandra Day, 114
Ohmae, K., 101
O'Mara, J., 13, 14, 15
O'Neal, M., 84-85
O'Reilly, C., 75
Organization(s):
  performance issues, 72-81
  protecting integrity of, 16
Organizational culture, see Corporate culture
Organizational ethics:
  codes of, 14-15, 59-61, 102-103
  cultural values and, 55-56
Organizational goals:
  economic, 74
  health-related, 74
  subcultures and, 35
Organizational perspective, on ethics and
    human diversity,
    6-7
Ouchi, W., 34

Packer, A., 12
Palmer, A. T., 87
Pant, L. W., 15-16
Paralanguage, 19
Pascale, R. T., 95
Past orientation, 37
Payne, R. L., 99
Peale, N. V., 111
Pearce, J. A., 75
Peers, learning ethical behavior from, 48, 97
Performance evaluations, 125, 128-130
Performance issues, 72-81, 138-141
Permutter, H. V., 88
Personal standards, 28
Pettit, J. D., Jr., 26, 36, 61
Petty, R. E., 58

Pillsbury, 21
Pluralism, 8
Political contributions, 60
Population growth, immigration causing, 9
Porter, L. W., 80
Posner, B. Z., 61, 62, 104
Post, J. E., 18
Power, C., 13
Power distance, 46, 47-48
  cultural clusters and, 53
  guidance in ethical conduct and, 97
  work ethic and, 81
Pragmatic value orientation, 91
Predictability, Japanese culture and, 39
Prescriptive ethics, 24
Primeaux, P., 35
Principles, ethical standards based on, 26, 27
Procedural justice, 31
Professions, homosexuals in, 14
Profits, 21, 73
Promotions, 12
  minorities, 83, 84, 85-86
  white males, 86-87
  women, 84, 85, 89
Protestant religions:
  accumulation of wealth and, 36
  work ethic and, 80
Protocol:
  East Indian culture and, 40
  Western European value system and, 42
Psychological immersion in work, 75
Pugh, D. S., 99
Pulley, K. J., 26, 36, 61

Questioning, American value system and, 44

Racal-Vadic, 69
Race, 5
Racial differences, 35
Racial-related conflicts, 148-149
Randall, D. M., 77
Rawls, J., 31, 83
Reactive ethnic identity, 59
Reasoning process, in applying ethical codes,
  25
Recruiting:
  corporate culture and, 58

human resources management and, 95-102
Regulating ethics:
  through corporate culture, 57-58
  through hiring process, 101-102
Regulatory pressures, 22
Reichardt, K. E., 61
Reidenbach, R. E., 17, 50, 97
Relativism, *see* Moral relativism
Religion, 3, 5, 36
  Asian, 38
  Eastern European value system and, 41
  freedom to practice, 132-137
  Latin culture and, 40
  Western European value system and, 42
  work ethic and, 80
  See also Islamic culture; Judaism;
    Protestant
Religions; Roman Catholic religion
Religious beliefs, sexual orientation and, 14
Residence, place of, 3, 5
Reverse discrimination, 120
Reynolds, L., 80
Right (political), family values and, 14
Rights, 31-32
  employee, 83
  foreign-owned companies and, 88-89
  gay, 7
  moral, 83
  promotions and, 87
Robin, D. P., 17, 50, 97
Robinson, R. B., 75
Rokeach, M., 24
Role relativism, 28
Roman Catholic religion:
  France and, 42
  Latin culture and, 40
Ross, D., 13
Rules:
  Australian value system and, 43
  corporate culture and, 17
  ethical standards based on, 26, 27
  Western European organizations and, 43
Russia, Eastern European value system and,
  41

Sanders, G., 34
Schauffler, R., 58
Schein, E., 19, 34, 75

Schermerhorn, J. R., Jr., 31
Schilling, M., 89
Schlesinger, A. M., Jr., 8
Schmidt, W. H., 61, 62, 104
Schroeder, D. L., 61
Schuler, R. S., 95
Schwartz, H., 75
Segal, T., 85, 86
Service sector jobs, work ethic and, 80
Setting, deriving meaning from, 19
Sexual diversity, defined, 5
Sexual orientation, 3, 14
Shafritz, J. M., 105, 106
Sharp, D. J., 15-16
Sheedy, J., 80
Shimko, B. W., 80, 81
Shintoism, 38
Siehl, C., 34
Sikhism, 40
Simon, H. A., 75
Sims, H. P., 50, 97
Sims, R. R., 103
Sinclair, A., 34, 57
Singer, A., 76, 83
Sisk, H. L., 91
Skinner, S. J., 49, 97
Smart, T., 85, 86
Social class, *see* Social position
Social group relativism, 29
Social information processing, 18
Social interaction, Asian cultures and, 38
Social issues, responsiveness to, 108
Socialization, in corporate culture, 101
Social order, Western European
  organizations and, 43
Social position, 3
  Australian values and, 44
  East Indian culture and, 40
  French value system and, 43
  Japanese culture and, 39
  Latin culture and, 40
Social pressures, corporate responses to, 108
Social responsibility, 21-22, 107-108
Social responsiveness, 108-110
Social roles, 28-29
Social trends, sensitivity to, 62
Societal perspective, on ethics and cultural
  diversity, 4-6
Soloman, C. M., 18, 87

South America, immigration from, 10
Spiritual diversity, defined, 5
Sprint Corporation, 109
Standards, 24
    corporate culture, 57
    personal, 28
State Farm Insurance, 21
States, immigrants settling in, 10-11
Status:
    British value system and, 43
    French value system and, 43
    See also Social position
Status descriptors, 3
Steers, R. M., 76
Stein, Daniel, 4
Steiner, G. A., 76
Stewart, J., 7, 14, 19
Stoner, J. A., 61
Strategic plan, 111
Strategy implementation, organizational
        performance and, 72,
    73, 74-77
Subcultures, 58
    American, 44-46
    coalitions of, 34
    organizational goals and, 35
Subordinate-superior relationships, 47-48
Superogatory duties, 21
Supervisors, role reinforcing ethical behavior,
        103-104
Supreme Court:
    affirmative action and, 114
    gay rights and, 7
Swartz, J., 7
Szilagyi, A. D., Jr., 74

Taciturn demeanor, in Asian cultures, 38
Taoism, 38
Teaching values, corporate culture and, 17
Team productivity, foreign nationals and,
        138-141
Technical workers, shortage of, 139
Telemarketing, ethics and, 109-110
Teleological perspective, 26
    managerial values and, 91
Termination decisions, 125-127, 129
Time orientation, 37
    American value system and, 44

Eastern European value system and, 41-42
    East Indian culture and, 40
    Latin culture and, 41
    Western European value system and, 42
Timing, deriving meaning and, 19
Tolerance, 30, 35, 62
Toobin, J., 7, 114
Tradition:
    British value system and, 43
    French value system and, 43
Training:
    corporate culture, 58, 101
    diversity, 19
    ethics, 60-61, 103
Transsexuals, 5
Transvestism, 5
Tribe, L., 7
Tunstall, W. B., 57

Ulrich, T. A., 104
Uncertainty avoidance, 46, 47, 48-49
    achievement motivation and, 81
    cultural clusters and, 53
    unethical conduct and, 97
Unethical behavior:
    cultural dimension effects, 97-98
    employee commitment effects, 76-77
United States, see America
US Corp., 21
Utilitarianism, 31

Values:
    core, 19
    conflicting, 68-69
    corporate culture, 57
    differences, 19
    economic, 91
    ethics and, 24-25
    managerial, 90-92
    social roles and, 28
Values of others, accepting, 62
Value systems, cultural, 37-46
Vaught, B., 26, 36, 61
Velasquez, M. G., 15, 92
Vincze, J. W., 74
Vitell, S., 104
Vitell, S. J., 49

Vogel, D., 15, 27

Wallace, M. J., Jr., 74
Washington, George, 36
Wealth, accumulation of, 36
Weber, J., 85, 86
Weick, K. E., 99
Werhane, P. H., 31
Western European cultures, 42-43
  dimensions of, 47
Western society, Bible and, 36
Western standards, 62
Western values, 35
White males:
  hiring, 86-87, 142-143
  promoting, 12, 86-87
Wilkins, A., 34
Williams, J. C., 91
Wines, W. A., 61
Wisdom, J., 28
Wolin, S. S., 27
Women:
  on boards of directors, 110
  hiring, 84, 88, 120, 143-145

Latin culture and, 40
  promoting, 84, 85, 89
  retaining, 85
  in workforce, 12, 87
Women managers, Japanese organizations
  and, 39
Wood, D. J., 31
Work, involvement in, 75
Work attitudes, 79-81
Work ethic, 79-81
Workforce:
  demographics, 8-14
  rate of adding diverse individuals to,
    64-70
Wright, P., 77
Written codes of ethics, 60, 102

Yang, D. J., 13

Zeiger, D., 12
Zen Buddhism, 39
Zey-Ferrell, M., 48, 97
Zinn, L., 13

About the Author

Willie E. Hopkins (Ph.D., University of Colorado) is Associate Professor of management at Colorado State University. He has published over 30 articles, many related to ethics and diversity, appearing in journals such as the *Journal of Business Ethics, Journal of Managerial Issues, Management Quarterly, SAM Advanced Management Journal, International Journal of Management, Human Resource Management, Business & Society, Public Personnel Management,* and several other HRM and strategy journals. Along with teaching in executive MBA programs in both Denver and Fort Collins, Colorado, he periodically conducts diversity training and seminars for Hewlett-Packard and the Washington State Department of Transportation.

About the Case Contributors

David B. Balkin (Ph.D., University of Minnesota) is an associate professor of management at the University of Colorado at Boulder. He has published over 35 articles appearing in such journals as the *Academy of Management Journal, Strategic Management Journal, Industrial Relations, Personnel Psychology, Journal of Labor Research,* and the *Academy of Management Executive.* He has also written or edited three books on HRM topics.

Minnette Bumpus (Ph.D., University of South Carolina) is an assistant professor of management at the University of Colorado at Boulder. She holds professional memberships in the Academy of Management, the North American Case Research Association, the Society for Case Research, and the Western Casewriters Association. Her current research interests include leadership, ethics, and diversity in the workplace.

Shirley A. Hopkins (Ph.D., University of Colorado) is an associate professor of statistics and operations technology at the Daniels College of Business of the University of Denver. She has extensive managerial experience in banking and other financial institutions, has published a number of journal articles, and consults with companies on implementing operations technology. She is a member of the Decision Sciences Institute, and her current research interests include service quality, productivity in service operations, and diversity.

Wilfred J. Lucas (MBA, Harvard University) is currently vice president/general manager of the Dealer Management Group of Baxter Healthcare Corporation. He is a trustee of the board of Mt. Sinai Hospital Medical Center in Chicago and serves on the board of directors of the Chicago Regional Purchasing Council.

Winter Nie (Ph.D., University of Utah) is an assistant professor of management at Colorado State University where she teaches in the area of operations management. She is coauthor of a book on managing global operations and has published in the *Journal of Operations Management, Journal of Production and Inventory Management, Journal of Asian Business,* and the *Journal of Management and Entrepreneurship.* Her research interests include service operations and international operations management.

DATE DUE

APR 1 6 2002		
GAYLORD		PRINTED IN U.S.A.